EAGER
for the
MASTER

Spiritual Lessons Learned
from Man's Best Friend

EAGER
for the
MASTER

Spiritual Lessons Learned
from Man's Best Friend

BART CHRISTIAN

Niche Pressworks

Eager For the Master

ISBN-13: 978-1-952654-52-7 Paperback
978-1-952654-55-8 Hardback
978-1-952654-54-1 eBook

For permission to reprint portions of this content, or for bulk purchases, contact Bart@BartChristian.com

Published by Niche Pressworks; http://NichePressworks.com
Indianapolis, IN

The views expressed herein are solely those of the author and do not necessarily reflect the views of the publisher.

DEDICATION

To my beautiful "girlfriend" for four decades, Melisa Leigh. From the moment she said, "I do," her smile, gentle spirit, and loving devotion have given me the greatest earthly joy I could ever have desired. Her patience when I work late, her encouragement when I am feeling anxious, and her touch when I need it most have held me together for the better part of my life. Despite every pain and grief, I have ever caused her, she has returned to me with love and blessing one thousand-fold. The greatest of these blessings were our two beautiful children and a home held together by God's grace and her love.

An excellent wife, who can find?
She is far more precious than jewels.
The heart of her husband trusts in her,
and he will have no lack of gain.
She does him good, and not harm,
all the days of her life.
— PROVERBS 31:10–12 (ESV)

CONTENTS

CHOOSING SOMETHING GOOD

In my adventure novel, *Into the Vortex: A Tale of Resiliency*, I make the case that resiliency and hope are core attributes necessary for leading a full and enriching life. As the saying goes, life is good, but it is full of challenge and adversity. Along the path of life, we must choose carefully what and who to take with us. From a faith perspective, our choice is clear. Faith, hope, and love are three undeniable virtues that will aid one through the most adverse circumstances.

As a longtime friend and colleague, I was intrigued and excited when Bart Christian provided me with a copy of his most recent book, *Eager for the Master*. Bart and I have a long and fascinating history that was born out of tragedy after the unexpected death of a close friend, Kevin Renfro. Such losses are often inexplicable and cause careful examination of one's soul for guidance and understanding. Our friend Kevin was a uniquely gifted person who put God, family, and friends first in life. His dog "Sugar Bear" was an important member of his family and helped cement the love between parents and children. Likewise, Bart's love of and appreciation for animals, especially horses and dogs, have played an important role in his life. This became especially clear when he and his wife Melisa added a wonderful German Shephard puppy Reign to their family in August 2020. Reign, who was aptly named on many levels, became their "dog daughter" and would help them see their world from a new perspective, one of faith, hope, and love!

My wife, JoAnne, often says, "Out of everything bad comes something good." Such was the case for Bart as he moved forward in life to overcome the loss of his best friend, with whom Bart had also been planning a business venture. Loss of a loved one can serve as a catalyst to move forward in life or spiral downward into an emotional abyss. To Bart's credit, he moved forward with determination and enthusiasm and became an innovator and motivator in the food service industry as well as a nationally recognized speaker. He also wrote a series of books to help others become more effective communicators, problem solvers and innovators.

Eager for the Master is a unique and wonderfully woven book that provides the reader with 28 lessons in seven subject areas. The core message is about God and relationship, and how our canine companions often illustrate the best and clearest examples of how we are supposed to lead our lives. Although other authors have attempted to capture these parallels, Bart provides a depth and breadth of knowledge that leaves the reader pondering clever and practical insights. Application is key, and most readers will completely reexamine their relationship with God and their relationships with dogs and others in unique and fulfilling ways! In the end, I suppose there is a reason that GOD is D-O-G spelled backwards. No one explains this better than Bart Christian! Well done, and thank you, my friend!

In Christ,
John Poidevant, Ph.D.
President, Resilient Horizons
Author of *Into the Vortex, A Tale of Resiliency* (Greenleaf Book Club)

FIRST DAY AT HOME WITH US

INTRODUCTION

Every morning, it is the same story. We wake up to the alarm buzzing, the birds chirping, and the sun peeking through the blinds. As I slowly slide out from under the warm covers, I am greeted by the furry back of Reign, our beautiful female German Shepherd. She refuses to let me touch the floor without first getting a belly rub with my feet. Then, with wet licks, excitement, and groans of love, she demands our attention and affection to start her day.

She is persistent, unrelenting, and as you probably guessed, she gets everything she wants. Why? Two really simple reasons: She does not give up, and we love her.

We have come to recognize that Reign understands her complete reliance on us. Is she always "good"? No, she is not. She barks, jumps on visitors, and occasionally has an accident in the house.

There is no doubt she knows exactly when she is bad. When she has done something wrong, she either lovingly submits to us or hides from us. She also has a habit of bringing in from the desert "gifts" that are usually either prickly or worse. Her odd habits can make her a bit obnoxious, often falling short of what we want her to be. Yet, we still love her.

She also loves us. She follows us everywhere in the house and is constantly in our path. She is sad when we leave and goes absolutely nuts when we come back home. She can't get enough of us. She never wants to be separated from us, wanting only to bask in our presence.

Do we need her to survive? No, we absolutely do not. Do we beg for her affection? No, we do not. Does her coming to us freely to offer her submissive love and undemanding affection make our world brighter? Yes, in almost every way. Her relationship with us is special, and it has taught us so much about ourselves and how lonely this life could be without this dog constantly in our faces.

In fact, this volume offers to you 28 lessons, in seven subject areas, that this amazing dog has taught me about how God, by His grace, loves and cares for us. There are also topics that address how we are to love and seek Him each day. This is about the relationship we are called to seek with the Creator and the blessings that relationship promises.

Reign is forever "eager for the master." That is what this book is all about. We, too, have a Master who loves us, cares about us, and wants to bless us continually—but there is a catch. We must desire to be in His presence and be listening for His call. In short, to obtain the full measure of the Master's love, we must be eager to be in His presence.

O God, you are my God, earnestly I seek you;
I thirst for you, my whole being longs for you, in a
dry and parched land where there is no water.
I have seen you in the sanctuary and beheld your
power and your glory.
Because your love is better than life, my lips will glorify you.

— PSALM 63:1-3 (NIV)

DAILY REUNION

REIGN AND BIG BROTHER, MAVERICK

Chapter 1

MORNING GREETING

Reign's "morning greeting" is absolutely all about pleasing us and letting us know that she loves us without reservation. It is really kind of magical, and we look forward to it as much as she does.

In the morning darkness, she becomes a mobile obstacle course as we try to make our way through the bedroom. We never really encourage her eagerness. It's just how she is.

To her, yesterday's misdeeds, intentional or not, are forgotten. Gone is the fact that she purposely dug out and chewed up papers from my office wastebasket to protest our leaving her home alone for too long. Her unintentional "excitement tinkle" on the floor when we got home is a thing of the past... and so is her responsibility for the scratch she accidentally left on my bare foot when she stepped on it (even though the scratch is still there). Each day brings a newness and joy for her. All the baggage, pains, and trials of yesterday are long gone, and this day, for her and us, is a brand new one in every way.

There is no tally, no scoreboard of past misdeeds, just a blank slate with endless opportunity and promise, beginning with her at our feet and craving our affection.

Our relationship with God is much the same way. Oftentimes, He waits for us to make the step toward Him before reaching down and laying His hand of comfort on us. He is always there, never far away, ready to give abundantly to those who will simply be joyful, faithful, and eager to be with Him.

Our tone for the day, our decision to be joyful (or not), all starts in the morning. David wrote, "Let the morning bring me word of Your unfailing love" (Psalm 143:8, NIV). If things are weighing heavily on your heart as you arise, go ahead and give those burdens over to the Lord. Commit to trusting Him and ask in faith for His wisdom to guide the decisions you have to make.

> The most critical part of any day, the moments that set your course, are the first fifteen minutes after you get up.

The most critical part of any day, the moments that set your course, are the first fifteen minutes after you get up. Do you awake with a "Thank you, Lord, for another day" mindset, or are you first thoughts, "Oh, God, not another day!"?

Our Father will not let us down, but it is our responsibility to ask Him to help us to get up. This begins each morning with thanksgiving and a faith in the promise the day holds. Expectation is a powerful, self-fulfilling prophet. If we expect the day to be bad, it likely will be just that. On the other hand, if we expect the day to be great and full of blessings, well, there is a pretty good chance we will be right.

Boldly thrust yourself into God's presence each morning when you rise. Pray expectant prayers for the very best of blessings during the day. I make you this guarantee: When things go your way (and they will more than not), your light will shine bright for everyone around you to see, and when things don't, that light will still shine. It will shine because you will know that the situation is not a stumbling block; it is a divine steppingstone to something special that is definitely there, just slightly out of sight.

If you boldly open the door to the Father in prayer and then quietly listen, you will likely be surprised and maybe even shocked at just how bold God can be in thrusting Himself and His greater blessing into your life. He doesn't compete with the world, and He holds more for you than you can imagine or dream. The catch, I believe, is that the first move toward Him is yours to make.

Reign never misses that first move. She is in our faces before we can even get out of bed, and she thrusts herself relentlessly into our paths to show that she loves us and trusts us to care for her. She knows that we will never let her down.

The truth is that we take great care of her. We give greater blessing (treats and playtime) when she deserves it and sometimes just because of her *dogged* persistence. She trusts that we will always watch over her. How much more do you think we can trust the Creator of Heaven and earth?

My voice You shall hear in the morning, O LORD.
In the morning I will direct it to You,
And I will look up.
— PSALM 5:3 (NKJV)

Let the morning bring me word of Your unfailing
love, for I have put my trust in You.
Show me the way I should go, for to You I entrust my life.
— PSALM 143:8 (NIV)

REFLECTION

- What is your morning attitude?

- What is your routine? Is it inspirational or is it demotivating?

- Do you set the tone for your day, or do you allow others to set it for you? Be honest.

Chapter 2

SMELLY SOCKS

Recently, we took Reign with us to a friend's house for a weekend getaway in the North Georgia mountains. After a great evening, we all called it a night and turned in. The next morning as everyone was waking up and assembling at the coffee maker, we noticed Reign in the corner of the living room lying on a big pile of socks.

Melisa and I knew right away what had happened. Overnight, Reign had gone room to room and retrieved everyone's dirty socks.

You see, our dog-daughter has one fetish that we just do not understand, and that is smelly socks. She loves 'em — not clean ones. No, she loves the ones that have been worn all day. You know, the socks that can be really *fragrant*.

She collects them by the pair (or more) and walks around the house triumphantly displaying them, eventually lying down on top of them. This time was no different, except now she had decided other people's socks were fair game, too.

We all laughed as she stood up, collected as many socks in her mouth as possible, and pranced over to the counter where the dog treats were stored. Promptly, she dropped all the socks, laid her chin on the counter, and stared at the treats in a jar, waiting to get what my wife calls the "morning sock bounty." The bounty was plentiful that day for sure.

It always puzzled us at first why she never went after the clean socks. Then it was so clear—they do not have our unique smell. The fragrant socks give her joy and comfort, allowing her to rest.

OK; I know you are wondering, "What do smelly socks have to do with God?" It's not about something being "smelly" but more about how the sense of smell itself can be likened to a spiritual sense. Each of our lives emits a certain "fragrance" to those we come into contact with each day. For some, it may be an odor of distrust, cynicism, anger, or fear, and yet there are those who have a fragrance of kindness, faithfulness, gentleness, and confidence. The truth is that your fragrance is infectious to everyone around you, be it fresh or foul, and it coats everything you do and say. You will draw those to you who want your particular fragrance and repel others who don't.

Each of our lives emits a certain "fragrance" to those we come into contact with each day.

I believe that in our spirits, we all crave the sweet aroma of love and confidence and seek it in whatever we do. But sometimes we seek it from the wrong things. So many in the world today are, as the old country saying goes, "lookin' in all the wrong places" for love and searching for confidence in a bottle or a pill. In every case, these futile endeavors lead us on a path we ultimately wish we had never taken. The evidence is all around us in our families, our workplaces, and the media.

This was never God's plan for us, and He grieves our poor choices. Yet, He gave us the free will to make our own decisions about the paths we take on the journey. His desire is that we seek Him first so He may show us the way, shower us with blessings as He will, and cover us with the fragrance of true love, real joy, and eternal confidence. God (Who, by the way, does not have smelly socks) has called us all to share the "pleasing fragrance" of His wisdom, joy, and peace with everyone we come into contact with, friend or foe. The reality is that we truly do gather from what we give to the world around us, and in many cases, we receive more abundantly than we gave.

Jesus declared to us, "Seek first the kingdom of God and all His righteousness, and all these things shall be added to you." Among these things is the sweet smell of confidence in whom we trust and a realization that He will cause all things to work for our best interests, as long as we hold tight to faith and belief in Him. God is good for His promises, and this is a big one.

Reign's love for our smell is just a small snapshot of what a true and meaningful relationship looks like with the God of the Universe, including the blessing He promises. We are to crave His attention and steal away every chance we can to listen for His whisper, and by doing so, we receive rest and comfort.

Now thanks be to God who always leads us in triumph in Christ, and through us diffuses the fragrance of His knowledge in every place. For we are to God the fragrance of Christ among those who are being saved and among those who are perishing.

— 2 CORINTHIANS 2:14–15 (NKJV)

Therefore be imitators of God, as beloved children. And walk in love, as Christ loved us and gave Himself up for us, a fragrant offering and sacrifice to God.

— EPHESIANS 5:1–2 (ESV)

REFLECTION

- What is the aroma you emanate to those around you?

- What is the one you crave most of all?

- Are you on a path that is creating a sweet aroma for those you encounter, or is it a stench that even you can't stand?

- Do you know that you can change it simply by your choices?

- Do you know how powerful you are in the presence of the Father?

Chapter 3

THE BALL

During one particularly important video presentation I was making to a group in the state of Washington via the internet, I had everything set perfectly. Lighting, camera position, and sound were all ready to go. I just missed one key step — I forgot to shut my office door completely.

We started on schedule with about thirty people in the meeting. The first half-hour went well, and then I stopped and asked the fatal question: "If there was one thing that you could stop today, what would it be?" I was expecting to open a discussion about potential negative habits and choices we all tend to make. Instead, thirty people shouted in near unison, "THE RAIN!"

I did not know my dog was lying just outside my slightly ajar office door, and they, of course, did not know her name was Reign. However, all she knew was that a lot of people had just called, and she needed to check it out, squeaky ball in mouth. She bounded in, jumped up in my lap (all fifty-plus pounds) and began squeaking that ball double time.

It was embarrassing, but it was also funny, and the audience insisted that Reign be allowed to stay in the room. I agreed, but the squeaky ball had to go. (To be honest, I think I eventually got that account because of the dog.)

Reign's desire to play with her favorite ball magnifies her persistence. Her ball, bright pink rubber with little soft spikes, has the most annoying squeaker built into it. We almost regret the decision to get it for her, and at times, we truly kind of hate it.

Of course, Reign loves it. When she is ready to play, she prances around the house with the ball in her mouth, poking us with it and incessantly squeaking it. Did I mention it was loud?

We bemoan the heat, the cold, the wind, and the rain... but we always relent and go outside to throw her ball while she joyfully chases it. We do our best to wear her out. But we never do.

Bottom line, we would likely never choose on our own to just get up and go out in the heat of the day or dead of night to throw that ball. Yet she keeps asking, knocking, and squeaking until we open the door and take time to play.

The Word gives us a pretty clear roadmap to being granted things that we need or want. It involves three simple steps — Ask, Seek, and Knock. The catch is that all three have a few strings attached.

Ask boldly, in faith and with a willingness to put in the effort required. You can ask all day long for a crop, but to reap a harvest, you must plant, water, and weed, or all the asking in the world will still yield nothing.

Seek diligently and consistently. Don't quit when the answers may lie just around the next corner. Don't give up seeking.

Remember: God's timing is not yours. I can imagine an angel standing ready to grant a blessing or request, and just at that moment, you quit. The angels then look at each and say, "Well, I guess they do not want this anymore. They just gave up seeking." Don't let that be your story.

Don't give up seeking. Remember: God's timing is not yours.

Knock and knock and knock. Keep asking boldly; keep seeking. Great reward seldom comes without faithful effort and commitment. Matthew 11:12 says that heaven is taken by violent men. This does not imply Rambo-type violence, but rather, it illustrates a committed persistence to keep banging on the doors of Heaven in bold and expectant prayer.

Here is a bonus tip that I have found to be true in my prayer life. So many times, we pray the problem over and over, giving it more and more power in our minds. It can go something like this: "Lord, help me to get over this (fill in the blank)," which we repeat every single day. It seems to get bigger and bigger. Why? Because we are magnifying the problem with every prayer we repeat.

There was a time in my prayer life where all I prayed was "God, help me with my business. It is not growing, and I do not know what to do. I need Your guidance." I prayed this prayer in some form for over a year and nothing really changed during that time. In some ways, my problems seemed to get bigger and worse.

Then one day, something came over me (now I believe it was the Holy Spirit) and I started praying a different prayer. I prayed, "Oh Lord, I thank you and praise You for the growth that I am being blessed with and the guidance You are giving me in my life and in my business. No matter what happens, I will be grateful and will trust completely in Your will for my life."

It wasn't overnight, for sure, but things began to turn around, and I truly believe it was a combination of my deciding to stop focusing on the struggle and turn not only my words but also my heart to total trust in the promise that God answers prayers. I just needed to change what I was praying over and over, and, as in all things, God has been true to His Word.

Try this out: pray for help once — that is right, ONCE. Then from that point on, only thank God for His deliverance from the problem and His divine intervention on your behalf. This magnifies the solution and the promises God has made in His Word. Jesus said, "And I will do whatever you ask in my name, so that the Father may be glorified in the Son" (John 14:13, NIV). God is glorified in answering your prayers, so incessantly pray the victory and let it, not the problem, get bigger.

We are called to ask, to seek, and to knock for those things we desire, to make our petitions known to God. He promises us many things in scriptures; however, He does not say that every request will be granted. What is promised is this: "And we know that all things work together for good to them that love the Lord" (Romans 8:28, KJV). If it is ultimately not going to be for our good, the request will not come, no matter how much we want or ask for it.

> If we are honest and look back on all our prayers, we all will see that sometimes what we wanted was not good for us.

If we are honest and look back on all our prayers, we all will see that sometimes what we wanted was not good for us. God reminds us in Isaiah 55:8 that His ways are not ours and our thoughts or desires are not His. If you have ever had children, you probably already understand that for their own good, sometimes you just have to deny them what they really want, "period, end of story," as a dear friend's dad used to tell us.

Do we always get what we want? No, we do not — just as when Reign wants something that we know would hurt her, we do not give it. She whines, cries, and keeps knock-knock-knocking, but it is just not going to happen because we love her and are committed to protecting her. We don't like it, but sometimes we have to disappoint her.

She eventually learns to change gears and focus on something else.

Sometimes we are just asking out of the wrong place or in the wrong time. When God does not answer, it does not necessarily mean "no;" sometimes it means "wait," or something like our feeling with Reign, "just not the squeaky ball."

Ask, and it shall be given you; seek, and ye shall
find; knock, and it shall be opened unto you.
— MATTHEW 7:7 (KJV)

Now to Him who is able to do exceedingly
abundantly above all that we ask or think,
according to the power that works within us.
— EPHESIANS 3:20 (NKJV)

REFLECTION

- What are you asking for and why?

- How are you seeking it each day?

- What kind of persistent knocking are you really doing?

- Are you magnifying the problem or the victorious solution when you pray?

Chapter 4

LICKS AND LOVE

Not too long ago, I pushed it a little too hard one weekend — spent too much time on a tractor and played a bit too
much on the lake all in the span of three days. I am not a "spring
chicken," as they say, and my back reminded me of that in no
uncertain terms. As a result, I spent three more days stretched
out on the sofa, alternating between an ice pack and a heating
pad to find relief.

During this time, my mood was kind of irritable (my wife may
have different adjectives for it), and it was funny how Reign knew
she needed to give me love versus begging for playtime or treats.

She lay at the end of the sofa, softly licking either my fingers
or toes. Her attention calmed me and helped me to rest. I could
almost see in her eyes that she was thinking, "You have taken great
care of me, and now it is my turn to care for you."

It was special, and in some way, I am sure it helped to relax me so I would heal faster, which I did. As soon as I was back on my feet, she quickly returned to her normal level of excitement to begin each day, which is far from gentle.

You really have not lived until a ten-month-old German Shepherd licks you from the tip of your chin to the top of your forehead, full contact and slimy all the way, in the dark at 5 a.m. Good morning kisses all around!

Reign is the most affectionately licking dog we have ever had, and we have had a few. She walks alongside us licking our fingers and hands; she licks our toes, feet, and legs; and of course, she does the sneaky, full contact slurp across the face. She constantly reinforces her love with us.

She acts as if there is nobody but us. Don't get me wrong; if something happened to us, she would absolutely be well cared for by our family. However, in her world, no one delights her more.

> "Delight yourself in the Lord, and He will give you the desires of your heart" (Psalm 37:4, ESV)

The Word tells us, "Delight yourself in the Lord, and He will give you the desires of your heart" (Psalm 37:4, ESV). The word "delight" is defined as something that brings great pleasure and satisfaction.[1] In this world, the media always seems to be moving the goalposts on what they think should bring us satisfaction, and the goal in most media outlets seems to be to deliver discontent and division to their audiences.

The Word of God gives us a different story, filled with promises of fulfillment, joy, and a "peace that passeth all understanding" (Philippians 4:7, KJV). Gaining this peace truly all depends on where you place the greatest desires in your life. If their source is in the material, your peace will fade and wear out regularly; if it is in the words of the intellectuals, you will be disappointed often; and if it is in your own strength, that will surely run out. True contentment is not found in this realm of mankind, and it never will be.

The most confusing thing to me is a discontented "believer" who reads the Bible daily, can quote scripture, and professes to be a person who prays to God every day, yet is still anxious and fearful about the temporary things of this world. For this person, it seems that even though they may have faith in God, their real trust lies within themselves and their finite ability to work things out on their own. What they are missing is the inescapable link between faith and trust. It is very difficult to experience the peace and deep joy of faith in God if you do not truly trust Him.

"The dog," as I lovingly call her, trusts us completely, and I think I know why. Immersed daily in our love and care, she does not know anything different. Her faith is complete, and she has no desire to allow any other person to compete with us for her trust.

It is very difficult to experience the peace and deep joy of faith in God if you do not truly trust Him.

My prayer for every believer who reads this is that you might strive to immerse yourself in the Word and cultivate a faith that trusts completely. I am certain that as you continue through this book, you will get this message a few times, but it is worth repeating: "Trust in the LORD with all your heart, and do not lean on your own understanding. In all your ways acknowledge Him, and He will make straight your paths" (Proverbs 3:5–6, ESV).

We give Reign every blessing we can that aligns with our plan (not hers) for her well-being, and she still wants only to be with us. Her faith and trust are set, and her joy is on full display for all to see. Oh, that others could see their lives as full of joy and peace because their trust lies not in their own ability but in the eternal promise of the Father, the Son, and the Holy Spirit.

Blessed is the one who makes the LORD his trust, who does not turn to the proud, to those who go astray after a lie!
— PSALM 40:4 (ESV)

Whom have I in heaven but You? And there is nothing on earth that I desire besides You.
— PSALM 73:25 (ESV)

REFLECTION

- Where are your desires and hope founded?
- Is that foundation bringing you a reliable stream of joy and peace to offset the chaos of this world?
- Is it time to re-evaluate and redefine where you have placed your hope and faith?
- Is it time to decide where your trust really lies?

TWO BABIES FIGURING IT OUT TOGETHER.

AFFECTION

BRINGING HOME A PRIZE

Chapter 5

UNDERNEATH THE DESK

There is truly something unique and special about a creature that simply wants to be with you. No ulterior motive and no requirements other than the need to be in your presence. This sums up Reign about 75 percent of the time.

When I am working on any project in my office, she has a habit of coming in and lying at my feet under the desk. When she is almost asleep, with either her chin, paw, or both lying softly on one of my feet, I glance down in these moments and know that she is not looking for any petting or scratches. She simply finds peace and refuge being near to me. I have to confess; I love it.

However, in other moments, all of the above are sort of out the window. These are the times when she brings in her favorite bone, lies at my feet, and crunches that bone incessantly while I am trying to concentrate. If I dare say anything to her like, "Please stop crunching that bone," she immediately stops and slowly begins to lick my feet or legs or hands, all the while circling my chair as if to say, "I am sorry for disturbing you." As irritating as she can be, I love these times, too.

There is no doubt that Reign sees the space under the desk at my feet as a refuge, a place of shelter or protection that can provide sanctuary from danger or distress. That is also exactly how God desires that we see Him. He is our refuge, our strength, and our very present help in times of trouble, and we can rely on that promise daily.

> He is our refuge, our strength, and our very present help in times of trouble, and we can rely on that promise daily.

There is a catch, though. If we want to truly feel the real refuge of God in our lives, we must live or dwell there. You may be scratching your head, wondering, "How exactly do I live with God?" The simple answer is, put yourself in His presence continually. Talk to Him when you arise in the morning, express gratitude at every opportunity, make at least a portion of every drive a chat with the Almighty, and when you close your eyes at night, give thanks for the lessons of the day.

I have to admit that Reign's near constant demand for my attention stretches my patience at times. I am, after all, an imperfect being with flaws and shortcomings.

Thankfully, our Father in Heaven does not have such flaws in His relationship with us. God has limitless patience, and He desires that we be in continuous praise and recognition of His glory. He is especially patient with, and shows special grace to, those who would routinely take refuge in His presence.

I know some may ask, "What do you mean by, 'thrust yourself into the presence of the Master'? Isn't God already aware of our needs?" The short answer is yes, God knows the deepest desires of our hearts, and yet Jesus shared many parables about persistence. In Luke 18:1–8, there was the relentless widow nagging the judge, and in Luke 11:5–15, a man badgers his friend into giving him a loaf of bread long after his friend has gone to bed.

In these stories, Jesus reminds us that it is by our persistence that many prayers are answered. As I mentioned before, He tells us very clearly to seek that we might find, ask that we might receive, and knock so that doors may be opened. All require our persistent action first in order for God to move in our lives.

David wrote in Psalm 27:4 (KJV), "One thing I desired of the LORD, that I will seek after; that I may dwell in the house of the LORD all the days of my life, to behold the beauty of the LORD, and to enquire in His temple." All David desired was just to be with God, to catch a glimpse and "inquire." Other versions translate this word as "meditate" or "seek." The bottom line is that he craved God and just wanted to fix his eyes and focus his mind on the glory of the Eternal One.

When she is with me in my office, Reign does not always want something. She does not really beg; she simply circles my desk, licks my leg, or just sleeps on my foot under the desk, all just to remind me that she is there and that she trusts me. She continuously craves any attention I might give.

Whoever dwells in the shelter of the Most High will rest in the shadow of the Almighty. I will say to the LORD, "He is my refuge and my fortress, my God, in whom I trust."

— PSALM 91: 1–2 (NIV)

Be thou my vision, O Lord of my heart; Naught be all else
to me, save that Thou art. Thou my best thought, by day or
by night, Waking or sleeping, Thy presence my light.

— ANCIENT IRISH HYMN[2]

REFLECTION

- Are you feeling a little disconnected or adrift in this world of man?

- Who or what is the presence you are dwelling in daily?

- Does it provide any meaningful peace or comfort to your heart and mind?

- Can you trust it to always be there as a help in times of trial?

Chapter 6

WHEN THE PACK IS INCOMPLETE

Let's talk about when this seemingly *perfect* dog goes utterly psycho for a few minutes. It happens whenever one of us leaves to run an errand or take a trip. It happens when we are separated for any length of time, all because she finds strength and peace with her pack.

One day as Melisa was preparing for her weekly trip to the grocery, the crazy in Reign emerged as she first stole Melisa's socks (surprise) and ran with them. After a short bout of "tug-o-war" with the socks, Melisa started to put them on. Sensing she was beat, Reign promptly laid on top of my wife's shoes.

After Melisa left, Reign frantically paced about the house, going from window to window, leaving little doggy nose prints on each as she gazed out sadly. Then she paced over to cry at the door. After a while, she skulked out of the room to hide somewhere until Melisa returned and we were all reunited, when Reign's world would be right again.

Something like this happens to both of us every time we are getting ready to leave. Bottom line, Reign does not want either of us to leave, ever. In her mind, the pack must stay together at all costs and at all times.

> *It is through our companions that we gain strength when our spiritual batteries are running dry.*

Reign, like any dog, finds strength and peace with her pack — and her pack happens to be my wife and me. Humans aren't much different. We also need a pack of people who share our concern for each other and whose beliefs at least somewhat align. It is through our companions that we gain strength when our spiritual batteries are running dry. It can be especially lonely when the weight of this world is getting heavier while our joy and peace begin to wear a little thin. Just like Reign, we all need a pack.

The Apostle Paul reminded us of this. He wrote, "Let us consider how to stir up one another to love and good works, not neglecting to meet together, as is the habit of some, but encouraging one another..." (Hebrews 10:24-25, ESV). Paul needed a pack, too.

The Father has built into most of us an instinct to seek and desire the company of other, like-minded people. The Bible is filled with stories of gatherings, celebrations, and parties where believers assemble together to gain strength and share their stories and testimonies, all while lifting up song, praise, or both to the Creator of the universe. By hearing how God has seen others just like us through this life's battles, we strengthen our faith and deepen our belief. Others let us know that we are not alone in our beliefs or our struggles.

Reign needs her pack, and more than anything, she wants to keep us together. She knows what we all know in our hearts: strength and power is amplified in numbers. That is what a congregation of believers can do for each other; they can turn up the volume of our faith if we will let them.

However, this applies equally to a "bad" pack that is cynical and negative, filled with complainers. They, too, will turn up the volume when gathered. If you have found yourself in a destructive group, it might be time to start looking for a new pack.

If you have found yourself in a destructive group, it might be time to start looking for a new pack.

But since we were torn away from you, brothers, for a short time, in person not in heart, we endeavored the more eagerly and with great desire to see you face to face...
1 THESSALONIANS 2:17 (ESV)

And let us consider how to stir up one another to love and good works, not neglecting to meet together, as is the habit of some, but encouraging one another, and all the more as you see the Day drawing near.
HEBREWS 10:24-25 (ESV)

REFLECTION

- Who is in your pack?

- Do they build you up, encourage you, and truly care about you?

- Does their presence bring negativity and stress, or joy and peace into your life?

- Do you desire to see them regularly?

Chapter 7

OUT FRONT—NOT REALLY

Reign loves to lead the way on walks, or just in and out of the doors to our home. It is kind of aggravating to have her stepping on my feet and giving me the "flat tire," or pulling the heel of my shoe off from behind. We deal with it because she likes to be in the front of the pack — or so she thinks.

Recently, we were in the backyard doing a little yard work. In classic form, Reign was first through the gate, but this time, we had a surprise for her. As she bounded past us, we gently closed the gate and hid from her just to see what would happen. As usual, she ran into the field full speed, greeted the horses… and then stopped, turned around, and began to run back and forth between our front and side gates, looking for us. She barked a couple of times, whimpered, and then just sat down. It was pretty clear that she felt suddenly lost by herself.

We quickly jumped up and called her. It was like we had been on a two-week vacation. She jumped, groaned, and made it really clear that she needed us. From that moment on, while we did our chores, she stuck to us tightly. We were not going to get another chance to sneak away that day.

God never hides from us; He is always there. However, we do make attempts to hide from or deny Him, especially when we know we have done wrong. This really has not changed much through time. In the Garden, when God was strolling about and calling, "Adam, where are you?", they were the ones who were hiding. God never left, and He always knew where they were.

In my life, I have had times when I did not feel the presence of God because I was ashamed of something I had done. I felt like I was not worthy, and therefore, somehow God was no longer there. I was scared that I had broken fellowship with Him and, of course, I was wrong. The promise He has made in some form over and over in the Word is, "I will never leave you or forsake you." Unlike man, God does not break His promises.

> The promise He has made in some form over and over in the Word is, "I will never leave you or forsake you." Unlike man, God does not break His promises.

We love to think we are strong on our own and do not need anyone, especially some god telling us what to do or think. The reality is that God, through the Word, really does not tell us what to think. He actually gives us the free will to think what we choose. The Word simply shows us the guideposts for greater joy and blessing along with access to the eternal. We decide to what degree we do or do not follow the path to greater blessing, peace, and grace.

Reign still beats us out the door and through the gate, but once through, she now pauses and glances back to be sure we are not far behind. We did not train or demand that; she chooses to do it because she understands that her security and joy are directly tied to how close she stays to us, her masters.

Therefore let him that thinks he stands
take heed lest he fall.
— 1 CORINTHIANS 10:12 (NKJV)

Pride goes before destruction,
and a haughty spirit before a fall.
— PROVERBS 16:18 (NIV)

REFLECTION

- Do you have an attitude that says, "I do not need anybody but me"?

- Are you hiding or running away from something?

- In the quiet places of your heart, is there a longing you just can't explain?

KINDA STILL A BABY

Chapter 8

DISCIPLINE

The really funny thing about Reign is that outside of the "potty training" phase, we have literally had to do very minimal disciplining. She does have an accident from time to time, but if you have ever had a young female dog, you know the "Oh, I am so excited to see you," tinkle is kind of to be expected.

Don't misunderstand. She will charge off into the desert chasing a rabbit, and we will yell at her, to no avail. Sadly, her failure to yield to our shouts often results in a nose or a paw full of cactus thorns. The desert has a way of exacting its own form of discipline without our help.

Our relationship with God is not much different, except in most cases, we know that what we are doing is not in our best interests, yet we do it anyway. In the movie *Scent of a Woman*, Al Pacino's character made a stirring speech, albeit profanity-laced, on honor and making the right choices. He said, "In my life I have come to the crossroads. I always knew what the right path was; without exception, I knew. But I never took it. You know why? It was too &@#$ hard."

> Oftentimes, the enemy of what we should do is what we want to do.

That is us. We almost always know the right path, but we don't take it. Why? It is either too hard, or it will require that we submit our pride or ego to something higher. Oftentimes, the enemy of what we should do is what we want to do.

God, in His infinite grace and wisdom, gives us that freedom but not without cost or penalty. Just like the desert, the universe has a way of exacting discipline when we ignore the stop signs. Our challenge is to let go of our fleshly desires and listen to the heavenly call to be our best selves. This requires humility and a release of our ego and pride.

Reign seems to understand, most of the time, that what she wants is often not what we want for her. Do we spoil her? Do we let her make her own mistakes? Do we sometimes let her wander into uncertain territory? Yes, on all counts. Does she listen when we tell her no most times? No. And when she doesn't, it sometimes causes her pain, and we allow that. We want her to learn.

God does not wish to control us; He wishes that we would trust and listen to Him so He can protect us from the "thorns" that surround us. We, like Reign, have decided that it is best to listen and avoid the "prickly" stuff as much as we can. You can, too; it is just a decision away.

And your ears shall hear a word behind you, saying,
"This is the way, walk in it," when you turn to
the right or when you turn to the left.

— ISAIAH 30:21 (ESV)

"For My thoughts are not your thoughts, neither are
your ways My ways," declares the LORD.
"As the heavens are higher than the earth, so
are My ways higher than your ways
and My thoughts than your thoughts."

ISAIAH 55: 8–9 (NIV)

REFLECTION

- Do you ever pray for roadblocks in your life to keep you from bad decisions?

- When something does not go your way, do you ever consider that not getting what you wanted might have been a gift?

- Can you recall a time when an unanswered prayer or a "no" from God was a blessing in disguise?

OBEDIENCE

THERE IS ALWAYS TIME FOR A TREAT!

Chapter 9

TREATS

One thing that Reign clearly understands is treats of all kinds. Whether it's a bone, chicken jerky, or just scraps from the table, she constantly wants more. To be honest, she gets a lot, but not all the time. As much as she desires them, we know she does not always need or deserve them.

As is our common provision with any of our horses, chickens, cats, and dogs, Reign always gets what she needs—food, water, and shelter. We never hold these back, and we give them equally to our most obedient and least cooperative animals. There is no withholding the basic needs, ever.

When it comes to what everyone needs, God handles us in much the same manner, in the form of common grace. It is given to everyone, whether they believe or not. It manifests in things like air, water, sunshine, rain, and to some degree, opportunity. He causes the bad man's crops to thrive just as much as the good man's, and likewise when the weather wipes a crop out. The Father is no respecter of persons in this regard; we are all given a relatively similar field to work in. We endure trials, we celebrate victories, and we have times when things are just okay. Common grace applies to all.

Then there is "blessing," which is defined as "God's favor and protection."[3] This is something that, while not necessarily always earned, it is the result of faithfulness and obedience. Solomon wrote in Psalm 37:4 (ESV), "Delight yourself also in the LORD, and He shall give you the desires of your heart." The one who "delights in the Lord" is not perfect, but his trust is sure, his faith solid, and the Lord in Heaven sees it, protects it, and rewards it.

So many see this verse as the "cookie jar" to God's blessing and getting what they want. Nothing could be farther from the truth. The reality is that when we delight in the Lord our desires change. No longer do we place our material needs first; true delight reveals to us the greater blessing the Father holds for us. Our desires and His begin to coincide and He reveals to us what we really want, the desire to know Him more.

> When we delight in the Lord, He likewise then delights in us.

"Delight" is a very interesting word because it alludes to a reciprocal emotion. It is defined as, "something that gives great pleasure" and "the power of affording great pleasure."[4] In essence, it implies both reaping and sowing at the same time.

Simply put, when we find delight in the Lord, it unleashes His power to "afford great pleasure" to us beyond common grace. This brings glory to the Father and opens the door to greater blessing, His favor and protection. When we delight in the Lord, He likewise then delights in us.

Reign delights in our presence. We reward that with greater blessing when she is obedient. We also do it sometimes when she is not so good because she routinely demonstrates her love and is obedient most of the time.

God does that with us, too. He knows our hearts, He knows our faith, and He blesses us sometimes even though we may fall away for a short time. Why? Simple, He knows who loves Him, and for some incomprehensible reason, He loves us more than we can imagine.

> *Blessed is the one who trusts in the LORD and whose confidence is in Him. They will be like a tree planted by the water, that sends out its roots by the stream. It does not fear when heat comes; its leaves are always green. It has no worries in a year of drought and never fails to bear fruit.*
>
> — JEREMIAH 17:7–8 (NIV)

> *Because he holds fast to Me in love, I will deliver him; I will protect him, because he knows My Name. When he calls to Me, I will answer him; I will be with him in trouble; I will rescue him and honor him. With long life I will satisfy him and show him My salvation.*
>
> — PSALM 91:14–16 (ESV)

REFLECTION

- Are there areas where you are struggling and need a little extra treat in the form of God's direction?

- When you ask, are you trusting Him for the answer?

- Do you set aside quiet time so you can hear His leading? Remember, God does not compete with YouTube or the Oprah Channel.

Chapter 10

COMPLETE LOVE

How can we describe complete, unconditional love? Reign has given us a lot of insight into what it means to love without exception. Are we perfect masters for her? No. Far from it, actually. When we first got her, one of us (me) was a little impatient and intolerant when she had accidents or got a little too joyful when we came home or a neighbor showed up at our door. She was kind of wild and crazy at times.

Sometimes there might have been a little yelling or a swat on the behind just to calm her down. It worked, but the reality is that there was probably a better way. The interesting thing is that Reign never changed her love or desire for me. In fact, she may have been more affectionate as a result. She knew she was out of line, and she knew that despite all my flaws, I loved, cared for, and would sacrifice for her. Her love for me was constant, complete, and unconditional.

Our Father in Heaven has a complete and unconditional love for His children. It is called *agape* love. *Agape* (ah-GAH-pey) is a Greek word that simply means selfless, sacrificial, and unconditional love granted by grace, with no measure of merit or favor. It is given just because. The good news is that unlike man, who is fraught with maladies like anger, selfishness, and impatience, God does not demonstrate these characteristics... thankfully. His love is patient, kind, and gentle, to name a few qualities. In short, it is a perfect love that He gives freely to the world in the form of common grace and lavishes in the form of blessings upon those called to Him by faith. It is unexplainable, and for those who will embrace it, eternal. Our God is truly awesome, forgiving, and in love with people, especially those who love Him.

> Our God is truly awesome, forgiving, and in love with people, especially those who love Him.

Does God chastise and discipline us? Yes, and deservedly so. The difference is that He never gives discipline in anger, selfishness, or impatience; it comes only from a place of love and a desire for our eternal well-being. God is definitely looking at the big picture and what is best for those who trust Him.

As a father of two children, I have had to make tough and unpopular decisions. My kids oftentimes wanted things that I knew were not in their best interests, and I had to say no. Sometimes that led to them being disobedient, and they required discipline. Why? Because I love them and my job as a father was to protect and provide for them.

Life had given me greater experience, and they did not or could not see the potential hazards that I did in what they wanted to do. It was my responsibility to keep them from harm where I could, especially when they were younger. It wasn't always popular, but God never called us to win a popularity contest with our children.

My son, who is a married man now with two children, sat down at dinner with me not very long ago and shared something that gave me great joy. He said, "Dad, you know, I think I am finally understanding." I replied, "Understanding what?' He said, "The things you did when I was young that I really did not like, I now see that you were only looking out for and protecting us the best you could. That was your job."

We are God's children. He is protecting us the best He can, and that best is only limited by our willingness to seek Him. Do we stray? Yes. Do we make bad decisions? Yes. To get our attention, our Father sometimes has to discipline us. Is it because He is angry or judgmental? No; it is because He is our Father. He loves us, and disciplining us is His job with those who will trust Him.

So, what about Reign, and how does this all fit together? I believe she draws closer to me after discipline because she trusts that I love her and will protect her as best as I can, no matter what. You see, Reign needs to know that the "alpha dog" (me) is watching out for her, protecting her, and when needed, lovingly correcting her. How much more will the Creator of the Universe and the indwelling Savior protect those who trust and love Him? It is truly incomprehensible.

The truth is that we humans also need an alpha for the very same reasons, and so many who are lost are following the wrong lead dog. As for me and my house, we shall follow, serve, and submit to the greatest and most trustworthy of all alphas, the "Alpha and Omega" of all, our Father in Heaven and Christ our Savior.

My child, do not despise the LORD's discipline or be
weary of his reproof, for the LORD reproves him whom
He loves, as a father the son in whom he delights.

— PROVERBS 3: 11-12 (ESV)

Blessed is the one whom God corrects; so do not
despise the discipline of the Almighty.

— JOB 5:17 (NIV)

REFLECTION

- Do you love someone unconditionally?

- Have you ever had to call them out and/or chastise them for bad behavior?

- Do you find it hard to accept that a loving God would discipline His children? Why?

Chapter 11

THE UNEXPECTED

One sure thing about Reign, she is constantly surprising us. She can be very unpredictable. Some days, she goes overboard lavishing love on us, and on others, she can be mischievous. On still others, she can be a little weird and distant. There are some days when she just doesn't eat anything and others when she devours everything and begs for more. She is, as my grandmother would say, "curious," meaning "odd."

The more we have grown to understand Reign, the less surprised we are when she has an odd day. As we have gotten to know her better, nothing really surprises us anymore. We know her heart by the love she demonstrates continually, and what we see as her sincere desire to be obedient is enough to overlook the quirky days when things go a little off the tracks.

I wonder sometimes how God must look at me on my curious days when I am not the person He has called me to be—when I say or do things that do not reflect upon Him very well. There are days when I think He must be disappointed or angry with my behavior or the unkind things I might say, and then it dawns on me that nothing I can do would surprise or shock Him. After all, He knows me better than I know myself.

He knows my heart and my faith. He loves me and sees that I love Him. There are no surprises, even when I am mired in what I might think is an unforgivable sin. The God of the Universe sent the ultimate sacrifice in Jesus Christ so those who are called to Him, who love Him and accept the free gift of salvation, might never again know an "unforgivable" sin.

> This gift of forgiveness to the believer has no strings. It does not expire, and it cannot be lost once it is accepted in genuine faith.

This gift of forgiveness to the believer has no strings. It does not expire, and it cannot be lost once it is accepted in genuine faith. It applies to the sins of the past, the disobedience of the present, and the times we will stray in the future. We can hobble our access to greater blessing above common grace, but there is nothing we (or anything else) can do that will separate us from His love and forgiveness. They are permanent and eternal.

The promise is this: "For as the heaven is high above the earth, so great is His mercy toward them that fear Him. As far as the east is from the west, so far has He removed our transgressions from us" (Psalm 103:11–12, KJV). The word "fear" cannot be misunderstood here. It is "profound reverence and awe,"[5] and transgressions mean any "infringement or violation" we may do is removed from our account and forgiven. Never forget that, unlike man, God keeps His promises forever.

Does Reign "mess up" from time to time? Has she broken something that in her eyes might be beyond repair? Does she know it when it happens? Based on how cleverly she can hide from us when an offense might happen, I have to believe the answer to all three is yes.

Our love for her never changes, and over time, we are less surprised at the few times when she does wander away from obedience. She can't lose our love; she can't lose our protection and our provision. She is ours, and we are hers, until the end.

That is exactly how our God and Savior sees us, and once our true faith is placed in Him, nothing can tear us apart from Him. Nothing we can do—past, present, or future—can separate us from God. We are His for the rest of this life and then for all eternity.

> *Nothing we can do—past, present, or future—can separate us from God.*

If we confess our sins, He is faithful and just to forgive us our sins and to cleanse us from all unrighteousness.

— I JOHN 1:9 (ESV)

For if you forgive other people when they sin against you, your heavenly Father will also forgive you.

— MATTHEW 6:14 (NIV)

REFLECTION

- Are you holding on to something you have done that seems unforgivable?

- Do you understand that through Christ, God forgave you long before you were even born?

- Are you holding a grudge against someone who has wronged you?

- Are you allowing this unforgiveness to create a barrier between you and God?

Chapter 12

FREEDOM

Many moons ago, our family had a husky named Koko. She was beautiful. Don't tell Reign, but I think she may have been the best-looking dog we have ever had. With her red coat, a blue eye, and a green eye, she was stunning, really, and she was a giant headache. She dug, she ran off, and she was completely disobedient 90 percent of the time.

We could not give her any freedom because the instant we did, she would run away. One time, she was gone for over a month and left a brand-new litter of puppies behind. Oh, I forgot to mention irresponsible, too. We loved her, but she was a pain in the... you know where.

Reign is different. She stays close, never runs off (except for chasing the occasional rabbit), and she just wants to be close to us. The result is that Reign has a lot of freedom whereas Koko had virtually none. We didn't love either of them any differently;

we just could not trust Koko with any greater freedom, for her own safety.

Through many parables in the Word, Jesus Christ would share stories about the connection between personal responsibility and greater blessing. My favorite is the "Parable of the Talents," found in Matthew 25:14–30. Three men were given varying amounts of money by their employer for them to put to work while he was away on a trip. Two of the men invested the money and made a return for their boss, but the third man was afraid he might lose it, so he buried his portion in the ground for safekeeping and earned nothing. The result was that the two men who had taken what was given to them and used it wisely were given more, and the one who hid his gift not only did not get more, but he also had his gift taken away.

God has given us all different and varying levels of talents in the form of spiritual gifts. Paul tells us:

Now there are varieties of gifts, but the same Spirit; and there are varieties of service, but the same Lord; and there are varieties of activities, but it is the same God who empowers them all in everyone. To each is given the manifestation of the Spirit for the common good. For to one is given through the Spirit the utterance of wisdom, and to another the utterance of knowledge according to the same Spirit, to another faith by the same Spirit, to another gifts of healing by the one Spirit, to another the working of miracles, to another prophecy, to another the ability to distinguish between spirits, to another various kinds of tongues, to another the interpretation of tongues. All these are empowered by one and the same Spirit, who apportions to each one individually as He wills" (1 Corinthians 12:4–11, ESV).

All who believe are blessed by the Holy Spirit with some spiritual talent to bring greater glory to God. Not all believers use them. Some bury them away, and to some degree, such gifts begin to fade. I am not sure that the cliché "Use it or lose it" applies, but I am certain the seed God has planted in you will never grow without your putting in the effort to cultivate it.

Paul also reminds us that the lack or abundance of fruit we yield is in direct proportion to the investment we make in its growth. He said, "But this I say: he who sows sparingly will also reap sparingly, and he who sows bountifully will also reap bountifully" (2 Corinthians 9:6, NKJV).

Proverbs 18:16 gives a promise to the person who diligently invests and grows the gifts God has given. "A person's gift makes room for him and brings him before great people." The more you grow the spiritual gift you have, the more doors will be opened for you to use it and the greater blessing can be bestowed.

In our materialistic world, we tend to interpret "blessing" as more stuff, but that is not the complete reality. Sometimes it does mean material blessing; however, many times, I have found that blessing has come mostly in the form of protection from harm, both physical and economic. For those who trust and "delight" in the Lord, He will always be sure to work things and events for our best interests.

> *The more you grow the spiritual gift you have, the more doors will be opened for you to use it and the greater blessing can be bestowed.*

Even though it may not seem that way at the time, if we trust Him, we will see it eventually.

We are all different in our level of faith and obedience, just like Koko and Reign. That does not change the Father's love, but it does affect the level of freedom and responsibility He gives to us. The more we obey and give trust to Him, the more He entrusts to us. It is really that simple.

The LORD makes firm the steps of the one who delights in Him; though he may stumble, he will not fall, for the LORD upholds him with his hand.

— PSALM 37:23-24 (NIV)

Walk in obedience to all that the LORD your God has commanded you, so that you may live and prosper and prolong your days in the land that you will possess.

— DEUTERONOMY 5:33 (NIV)

REFLECTION

- Is there an area where you could trust God's hand more?
- What is stopping you from giving that burden to Him?
- What steps could you take today to trust God more?

DID I MENTION THE BALL?

LOYALTY

FRIENDS WAITING TOGETHER

Chapter 13

ALERTS TO DANGER

When we first got Reign, she was a lousy watchdog. She knew no strangers and loved everyone. She was a puppy. It took her a little time to learn who she should trust and who would never leave her.

That all changed about the time she became nine months old. It was as if something awoke in her and she became a great watchdog. She still loves everyone, but she has developed a pretty keen sense of situations and can identify people who are just not right. Do we need her protection and alerts? In nearly every instance, the answer is no; however, we do appreciate that she demonstrates her love and trust by defending us when she thinks it is needed.

One morning while we were in the north Georgia mountains visiting our very best friends, John and Joanne, a very large black bear made its way into their backyard. Reign, along with Hobie, their Springer Spaniel, recognized the threat immediately and took action. Both charged the big bear and let it know that the welcome mat was definitely not out.

When it comes to defending our faith, many of us have become so numb to the sin in the world that we no longer recognize the spiritual dangers, or we just do not trust or believe enough in God to fight. Then there are the "infants" in faith, who just do not yet have a sense of how insidious and evil the enemy really can be.

More mature Christians are called to use the Word patiently to teach, rebuke, correct, and train others in right living so that they are properly equipped for the works God has laid out for them. One of those works is defending the faith so others might know the way to eternal peace and joy.

The Word gives us instruction and calls us to defend the faith. Here are a just a few examples:

- "Beloved, although I was very eager to write you about our common salvation, I found it necessary to write appealing to you to contend for the faith that was once for all delivered to the saints" (Jude 1:3, ESV).

- "… Always [be] prepared to make a defense to anyone who asks you for a reason for the hope that is in you; yet do it with gentleness and respect" (1 Peter 3:15, ESV).

- "[The believer] must hold firmly to the trustworthy message as it has been taught, so that he can encourage others by sound doctrine and refute those who oppose it" (Titus 1:9, NIV).

- "Preach the word; be prepared in season and out of season; correct, rebuke, and encourage—with great patience and careful instruction" (2 Timothy 4:2, NIV).

- "Have nothing to do with the fruitless deeds of darkness, but rather expose them" (Ephesians 5:11, NIV).

We are directed over and over again throughout the Bible, and particularly in the New Testament, to defend our faith. Like me, you may feel that when the time comes, you won't have the right words to say. God has made provision for that if we will just trust Him. Luke reminds us, "For the Holy Spirit will teach you in that very hour what you ought to say" (Luke 12:12, NKJV). That tells me that when I need the words to say, I will be inspired with them.

> "For the Holy Spirit will teach you in that very hour what you ought to say" (Luke 12:12, NKJV)

God does not need our defense, and yet, our faith in Him does. He reminds us of this throughout the Gospels. Our defense does bring Him glory, and yet when we openly stand against others' lies and attacks on our faith, it seems to bring us greater strength in our belief. The more we share what and why we believe, the more alert to dangers we become, and the deeper our faith becomes.

These attacks come in many forms. People we know and love, whom we have invited into our lives, may make subtle digs at our faith. Outside forces could try to subtly make their way into our minds through the media, or we could even face an all-out intrusion, like the bear who was trying to make its way onto the back porch. Regardless, our responsibility and our calling as believers is to be alert and gently rebuke those who would attack the truths found in God's Word.

Each time Reign gives us an alert and we respond, it seems that she grows more confident, stronger, and bolder in her senses. We love and praise her when she defends us, and we honor her willingness to stand up for us. God is no different. He honors those who guard and defend truth against this world's attacks.

> *The one who guards a fig tree will eat its fruit, and*
> *whoever protects their master will be honored.*
> — PROVERBS 27:18 (NIV)

> *Let love be without hypocrisy. Abhor [hate]*
> *what is evil. Cling to what is good.*
> — ROMANS 12:9 (NKJV)

REFLECTION

- Is there a time when you felt under attack by something or some force that you could not see?

- How did you feel during that time? Alone or protected? Weak or strong?

- Did you stand against it or run away?

Chapter 14

STRANGERS

Reign is definitely a loving dog, and honestly, she wants to share her love with everyone she meets. She is always looking to make new friends with an abundance of love and joy. Sometimes it is just a bit too abundant.

She licks and playfully jumps at everyone she meets, no matter where we take her. Walking her is a total body workout from just trying to hang on as she pulls and tugs to greet total strangers — many of whom do not share her exuberance for becoming friends.

This was on display the first time we took her to a dog-friendly outdoor restaurant. My first mistake was wrapping leash around one of our table legs, a choice that almost cost us two drinks and an appetizer when another dog walked by on the sidewalk.

Mistake number two was to tie her to the outdoor railing around the dining area by our table. Two little kids, maybe four and six years old, walked by our table (did I mention Reign LOVES kids?) and she almost pulled the railing out of the concrete to get to them. Fortunately, their parents were dog lovers and brought the little boy and girl over to see Reign. Disaster averted, thankfully.

One day, this changed when someone came up to the house trying to sell us his landscaping services. When he walked up to chat, I was outside, and Reign was in the house. In talking with the man, something seemed a little off to me, but no big deal. We needed some work done, and he seemed nice enough. So, we hired him for a few hours of yard work.

Just before he began working, Reign managed to get out the front door, and Melisa and I both thought, "Oh great, here we go with the licking, jumping, and excitement tinkles."

In typical fashion, she galloped joyfully toward the man as if everything was normal—and then stopped on a dime within about five feet. Backing up with the hair on her spine standing up, she did something we had never seen: She began to growl and show her teeth. She had finally met someone she did not like at all. Reign was letting us know something was not right, and we would later learn what it was.

The Word is full of references to "entertaining strangers," and in one verse, it reminds us that in doing so, we might actually be in the presence of angels without realizing it (Hebrews 13:2, ESV). Our clear call is to be open to meeting and welcoming people we do not know yet. We are to treat them well and not be immediately suspicious of their intentions.

Yet in the world of man, we must be discerning and wise. Discernment is defined as "the quality of being able to grasp [sense] and comprehend the obscure" in a person or situation.[6]

This is a tough thing for a lot of people because the common source for many is their own understanding and/or the picture of mankind painted in the media.

Solomon tells us in Proverbs 3:5–6 (NKJV), "Trust in the Lord; lean not on your own understanding." Simply said, many times we are not our best counselor; we need another source. He also goes on to write. "In all your ways, acknowledge [recognize] Him, and He shall direct your paths."

One powerful and often ignored tool we've been given is our intuition. It is simply that still, small voice that will guide us, more times than not, in the right direction. The problem with many is a tendency to react instantly and emotionally rather than taking a few seconds — literally a single deep breath — before acting. Many times, that slight pause and brief moment of reflection is the difference between a good or bad decision.

> *One powerful and often ignored tool we've been given is our intuition.*

This is especially true about strangers. They are, 99 percent of the time, good people, and if you will just ask God and trust Him for His discerning wisdom, He will grant it every time. He knows those who would cause harm, and He wants to guide us away from them. Our job is to have faith, pause, and ask for His direction.

In this case, Reign tried to warn us, but we did not listen and entered into a bad deal for the yard work. Work was not completed as promised and many things were shoddily done, to say the least. It cost us money, time, and temporarily dented our faith in humanity a bit. It was our fault for not listening, not Reign's, not really the man's, either, and for sure not God's. It all could have been avoided if we had just been a little more discerning and paid attention to what Reign was trying to tell us.

One thing is for sure, next time we will listen when Reign doesn't like someone and trust that maybe she sees something that we do not.

Do not neglect to show hospitality to strangers, for thereby some have entertained angels unawares.
— HEBREWS 13:2 (ESV)

If any of you lacks wisdom, you should ask God, who gives generously to all without finding fault, and it will be given to you.
— JAMES 1:5 (NIV)

REFLECTION

- Have you ever been let down by someone else?
- Did you see the signs early and yet do nothing?
- Did you blame the other person though you chose not to listen the Holy Spirit's guidance?
- Did you blame God?
- Did you take any responsibility for your choices?

Chapter 15

TRUST

Reign demonstrates her trust in us constantly. When it thunders, she runs to our side for protection; when she darts toward the road chasing something, and we yell, "No!" she stops. When we say "Come," she does, every time. (Full disclosure: it is "almost" every time; after all, she is a dog.)

Why does she trust us? I believe it is because we have never really done anything to damage that feeling. Have we let her make her own mistakes? Yes. Have we allowed her to wander in something that would cause her some pain? Absolutely. Yet every time, she comes running back to us for comfort and to relieve the pain. The funny thing is that every painful experience teaches her two valuable things: what not to do next time (hopefully), and the fact that she can trust us to be there when she comes back.

Trust is defined as an "assured reliance on the character, ability, strength, or truth of someone or something." This seems to clearly define not only how we believe Reign sees us, but also the relationship we are to have with our Heavenly Father — one of complete and unflinching trust in His good plan for our lives.[7]

Do we wander off in the weeds, rely on our own decision-making, and think we have all the answers from time to time? Absolutely and without exception, we all do. The interesting thing is that so many want to blame anything besides themselves for their bad decision-making and the unwise counsel they have been following. They just do not want to take responsibility for learning and practicing wisdom, and instead they blame everything else, including God.

I am reminded of a story of twin brothers, one a great father and very successful businessman, the other a deadbeat dad and raging alcoholic. A psychologist interviewed both in hopes of understanding how two men brought up at the same time, by the same parents, in the same household could turn out so dramatically different as adults.

The psychologist posed the same question to both: "What are the most impactful events you can point to that might have led you to the life you find yourself in today?"

The first brother, the alcoholic, deadbeat dad responded, "Well, you see, my mother was an abusive, drug-addicted woman who treated me and my brother horribly, and my dad was a violent alcoholic who was never around and left us when I was a teenager. The die seemed to have been cast before I was born. I had no choice but to turn out the way I have. My parents doomed me to this."

When asked the same question, the second brother, the successful business and family man, paused and dropped his head in thought, then said, "Well, you see, my mother was a drug addict and she treated me and my brother really bad, and our dad was an alcoholic who was also violent. I do not remember him being around much, and he finally left us when we were both just teenagers. I made the decision long ago to never let them condemn me to following in their footsteps. You see, I really had no choice but to break the cycle for myself and for my family."

There is much we can infer here, but the main point is that while one brother took ownership for his life and direction, the other placed blame and took little, if any, responsibility for the choices he had made.

Sadly, we all probably know someone who refuses to step back, take responsibility, and then step up and take ownership of the life they have made for themselves. I have heard it said that while life rarely gives us what we deserve, it almost always grants us what we earn.

Of course, things such as tragedy and illness seem unfair and lead many to question God and His plan. The variable that we are reluctant to address is the sinful condition of the world and how we compound that daily by a series of bad decisions that create conflict within us, between us, and with God Himself. Those who place their trust in this world and its rewards create a recipe for pain, disappointment, and confusion, as they must face the fact that the world seems not to fight evil but instead perpetuates it, and appears not to revile open sin, but instead celebrates it.

Those who place their trust in this world and its rewards create a recipe for pain, disappointment, and confusion.

Conversely, I have placed my trust in four simple truths:

- Father knows best. "But when you ask, you must believe [trust] and not doubt, because the one who doubts is like a wave of the sea, blown and tossed by the wind" (James 1:6, NIV).

- Don't question the power made available to you by God. "If you can?" said Jesus. "Everything is possible for one who believes" (Mark 9:23, NIV).

- The ultimate plan of God is trustworthy from the beginning. "Behold, I am with you and will keep you wherever you go, and will bring you back to this land. For I will not leave [forsake] you until I have done what I have promised you" (Genesis 28:15, ESV).

- The Master knows what He is doing. "Trust in the LORD with all your heart and lean not on your own understanding. In all your ways acknowledge Him, and He shall direct your paths" (Proverbs 3:5–6, NKJV).

Pretty straightforward, right? I know you have to be asking yourself, "Yes, but how does Reign fit in here?" Like this: When Reign wandered off into the desert the first couple of times and got a paw or nose full of cactus thorns, she ran from us and hid. Why? Because she knew removing the thorns would be painful, maybe more painful than getting stuck to begin with, and she wanted to avoid it.

She would actually make it worse on her own by trying to pull the thorns out with her mouth (which would cause her to get them in her nose), or scratching them out with her other paws, which didn't work, either. A bad situation just got worse when she tackled it on her own.

Her evolution has been very interesting, and it says a lot about spiritual maturity. Now, when she gets a thorn, she quickly seeks us out. She understands that while removing what she earned might be more painful, that is the only way to eliminate the pain altogether. The only relief would come through her trust and the touch of her master. Sound familiar?

For I know the plans I have for you, declares the LORD, plans
for welfare and not for evil, to give you a future and a hope.
— JEREMIAH 29:11 (ESV)

Have I not commanded you? Be strong and courageous.
Do not be afraid; do not be discouraged, for the LORD
your God will be with you wherever you go.
— JOSHUA 1:9 (NIV)

REFLECTION

- What are you earning from life?
- Are the choices you're making aligning themselves with what you want? Be honest.
- Are you taking full ownership and responsibility?
- Whose counsel are you listening to and trusting?
- Can you count on it being wise and in your best interest?

HIDING THE SHOES

Chapter 16

JUST SPEND TIME

Every time either of us leaves, Reign fights to make us stay—not with any malice, but certainly very passive-aggressively. This is no more on display than on Sunday morning as we both are getting ready to go to church. It starts with Reign blocking the shower by lying in front of it and then progresses to the game of "sock hide and go seek."

We feed her, but she pays no attention and only glares at us with a kind of pitiful disdain for what she knows is coming. As my wife walks in and sets her purse on the kitchen counter, I fill the water bowl and lay a couple of Reign's favorite treats, chicken jerky, on top of her food, but she pays them no mind, either.

"It's all right, girl," I tell her, "we'll be back soon; I promise." I give her a quick ear rub as I set her bowl on the floor. She doesn't look convinced. Feeling a pang of guilt, I stoop down and give her a full body rub and say, "Come on, now. Look, treats! You can't be sad with treats."

Reign whines and clearly does not agree. She can tell by how we have been bustling around getting dressed up that we are going somewhere, and she isn't. She does not care where we are going because she knows we are about to leave her alone. No amount of treats or food or soothing voices will take away the knowledge that the "pack" is about to be separated.

We do our best, but every Sunday (or any time we both leave for a few hours), it is some variation of the same theme. Like any good "dog parents," we leave her plenty of food, water, toys, and treats before heading out on whatever errand, visit, or appointment, only to find them untouched on our return. Only after Reign unleashes her usual joyful greeting on us when we come back, will she zoom into the kitchen to make up for lost time, gobbling up the treats first, then going for the food and water.

She seems to only want nourishment when we are there, after she knows we are all back together safely. We are the most important part of Reign's life, and she lets us know that every day.

As we all journey through this world, it is so easy to become detached from the things that are truly most important and to take for granted our spiritual nourishment. We forget to be grateful for our blessings, both great and small. The world's noise crowds out our mental clarity, and we find ourselves stressed, anxious, angry, over-weight, and unhealthy. Just like our bodies, our spirits need nourish-ment, too. The *perceived* challenge for many is simply finding the time.

I am always fascinated by those people who are not living any-where close to their best lives and are unwilling to consider that the problem is not that they have too little time; it is the fact they have too much time. They spend it on social media, watching television, watching the news (which is nearly all bad), and listening to the radio in the car while driving.

You may be thinking, "Changing these would not even make a dent in my time each day." Really?

Statistics show that the average American spends over one hour per day in their car, more than three hours watching television, and over two hours per day on a device of some type (smart phone, tablet or computer). That is more than six hours per day, Monday through Saturday, thirty-six hours a week.[8] You see? The real time problem is not too little time; it is too much.

Time is the real currency of life, and we never get back what is lost. However, we can all reinvest what we have left. A time inventory of a single day can reveal many surprises, and tracking an entire week might be shocking. We all have the

> *Time is the real currency of life, and we never get back what is lost.*

same twenty-four hours each day, with a limited amount left in our accounts. How are you spending or investing your life's time?

Just imagine what your world would look like if you fasted from all the above every other day and instead devoted that time to nourishing your soul and spirit. Redirect a portion of that time toward learning more, taking a walk, or exercising a bit, and make it about bringing yourself into the quiet presence of your Father in heaven.

So how in the world does this all relate to Reign? As I've mentioned before, she finds her real comfort, true peace, nourishment, and even her play, with us and us alone. In nearly every instance, we do not seek her out; she comes looking for us. She just wants us to spend time together.

Our Father in Heaven is much the same, in that He gives us all we need (not want) — the air we breathe, the water and food we take in, along with all the creation that surrounds us. Then He simply waits for those who desire His presence and love to come to Him. He does not compete with the noise of this world or force His love on us, and yet He lavishes love, joy, and peace freely upon those who will come to Him and just spend time in a true, humble, faithful spirit.

These words, written by Helen Lemmel more than a hundred years ago, are maybe needed more today than ever:

Turn your eyes upon Jesus

Look full in his wonderful face

And the things of earth will grow strangely dim

In the light of his glory and grace.[9]

> *Draw near to God and He will draw near to you.*
>
> — JAMES 4:8 (NKJV)

> *The LORD is near to all who call on Him,*
> *to all who call on Him in truth.*
>
> — PSALM 145:18 (NIV)

REFLECTION

- How are you spending your time?

- Have you taken a true time inventory?

- Is there time you could be spending differently?

- Where are you investing your life's time? In this world or the next?

FOOD, WATER,
AND CARE

ANYONE MISSING A SOCK?

Chapter 17

UNDER THE TABLE

If you have ever had a puppy, you know that one of the toughest things to break them of is constant begging for food of any kind: treats, cooking scraps, and leftover bites after dinner. Anything will do; they just want to get a bite of whatever they can, whenever they have the opportunity. Reign was no different; however, we did fix the begging by simply ignoring her when it wasn't the right time and rewarding her when she was obedient.

There is one habit that we still allow and that is her lying under the dinner table while we eat. She doesn't beg and lies very still. She just wants to be close enough so that if a crumb of some type does make it to the floor, she is ready to take advantage. To be completely honest, we purposefully will drop a bite in front of her from time to time, even though she has already had adequate food and water. Her humble and quiet desire just to be with us causes us to give her more beyond what she simply needs.

Our Father in Heaven treats His children in much the same way. He knows what we need and is faithful to provide it at the appropriate times. Our challenge is patience, obedience, and developing a habit of desiring His presence. As I've said previously, while common grace abounds for both the believer and those who are lost, the "above and beyond" blessings come in the times when we quietly stand on His promises and wait.

> We lift our prayers up not as "beggars," but as heirs in faith and expectation that God will answer them as He wills, and with our eternal best interests in His heart.

We lift our prayers up not as "beggars," but as heirs in faith and expectation that God will answer them as He wills, and with our eternal best interests in His heart. This oftentimes does not fit our timetable, and as a result, many descend into anger that God does not respond the way they think He should.

Job is a great example of someone who got angry with God when he said, "I cry out to you, God, but you do not answer; I stand up, but you merely look at me" (Job 30:20, NIV). Job covers his entire angry complaint against God in chapters 30 and 31, still God does not answer immediately. He waits.

In Job 38:2 (ESV), God answers Job, and to be honest, it is terrifying. The Father's reply begins with, "Who is this who darkens counsel by words without knowledge?" and it goes on from there, for two whole chapters. What Job did not understand in his anger and pain was that God had greater blessing on the way, beyond anything Job could imagine. Job was truly speaking without knowledge and was spiritually biting the hand that was feeding him. God had a different plan, a better plan for Job. The only requirements were perseverance, trust, patience, obedience, and a continued desire to be in the Master's presence.

Our stories, while maybe not as tragic as Job's started out to be, are very similar. Loss, pain, disease, sickness, and death surround us all. In Job, God lets us know that it is OK to get angry and even to challenge His plan, as long as our heart is right and our faith, though shaken, remains true. God had far better things in store for Job. He knew Job, His child, just had to find his way to it.

Job's story is our story too. He trusted the Master's heart, even when he could not understand His hand. This is the secret to seeing the promises of God's Word unfold in our lives. We must fight during the darkest of times to maintain our faith and trust because it seems that only in those times are we able to truly hear from God. This was true for the heroes of the Bible, and it is still true for us today.

Reign has never bitten me; she has never growled or expressed anger when she did not get what she wanted. She does get frustrated and she will, from time to time, pull all the stuffing out of a toy as a result. Yet she always is at our feet, loving and trusting that while she may not get the extra treat, there will be food and water in her bowl. She trusts that we will be there to meet her needs. That's why we give her the extras above and beyond what she needs, and in most cases what she desires.

> *We must fight during the darkest of times to maintain our faith and trust because it seems that only in those times are we able to truly hear from God.*

God treats us the same way. He sees your heart, knows your spirit, hears your prayers, and has promised never to leave or forsake you.

The challenge is to believe that unwavering promise no matter the situation. If we do, then just like Job, we will see the grace and love of our Father unfold in ways that we cannot imagine.

"Be still, and know that I am God."
— PSALM 46:10 (KJV)

"But rather seek the kingdom of God; and all these things shall be added unto you."
— LUKE 12:31 (KJV)

"Yes, Lord, yet even the dogs eat the crumbs that fall from their masters' table."
— MATTHEW 15:27 (ESV)

REFLECTION

- Are you angry with God?
- Have you reverently told Him or argued with Him?
- Have you taken time to be quiet, express your feelings in prayer, and then wait to hear?
- Are you expecting God to compete and speak to you over the noise and chaos of this world? If yes, is this expectation realistic?
- Is it time to stop fighting and just be still?

Chapter 18

PULL OUT THE THORNS, PLEASE

Like most dogs, Reign loves to explore. She never wanders far, but she does like to get off the trail to chase things she shouldn't. In Arizona, that can be treacherous. Barrels and cholla and saguaros… oh my! The cactus thorns are everywhere, and just waiting to bite you. It's kind of like life. When we stray off the path of our calling, the stickers are abundant.

I have mentioned before that at first, when Reign would get a thorn in her paw (or worse, in her nose or mouth), she would run from us. She knew she had done something she should not have done, and also that when we pulled the thorns out, she would have to submit and be patient, and that it could be quite painful. But the longer she hid and tried on her own to get them out, the worse her predicament became.

Watching her struggle, I realized that we are much the same. Removing the thorns we pick up from a life gone astray means we must find our way quietly to our knees and allow the Holy Spirit the opportunity to purge those things from our hearts and minds. In many cases, this is painful and really not something we want to endure. We run from God and try to work things out on our own, and the thorn only digs deeper into our lives.

Our Heavenly Father wants so much to help relieve the burden of the thoughts and sins we think we hide from Him. That is why He sent a Savior, His son, Jesus Christ. It was only through an ultimate, unmatchable sacrifice that He could release His Holy Spirit on those who would trust Him. Jesus called the Holy Spirit the Comforter because that is exactly what it is — our comfort and relief in (and from) the pain the world heaps on us or that we inflict on ourselves. The Holy Spirit is here to pull out the thorns where possible, and, if not, to give us comfort as we work them out according to God's plan.

The Apostle Paul cried out three times for God to relieve the "thorn in his flesh" (2 Corinthians 12:7-9), and God did not, because His plan was for Paul to experience His grace through it and to be humbled by his struggle. Sometimes it takes pain to help us finally seek God's face and feel His grace. We are, after all, a hard-headed people.

When Reign would get a thorn in her, we sometimes let her struggle and make it worse because otherwise, she would not submit for us to remove it — she would actually fight us. She didn't understand that we wanted to help. As a result, her pain increased.

Eventually, though, she began to come and lie down quietly at our feet so we could relieve her pain. Now, if you have ever been stuck with a cactus thorn, you know that pulling it out is, most of the time, a lot more painful than actually getting the initial prick.

However, once it is out, the pain goes away pretty quickly. Reign finally got that, but not before she experienced a lot of discomfort going it alone.

Our thorns are no different. They can sneak in with very little pain, but the longer they linger and deepen, the more still we have to be, and the more painful they are to remove. God does not compete with our emotions, our feelings, or the world to ease our pain. He requires us to humbly come to Him, to be quiet, and to embrace the pain we might require to be healed. His formula is really simple: "Be still, and know that I am God" (Psalm 46:10).

> *God does not compete with our emotions, our feelings, or the world to ease our pain.*

O LORD my God, I cried to you for help,
and you have healed me.
— PSALM 30:2 (ESV)

Heal me, LORD, and I will be healed;
save me and I will be saved,
for you are the one I praise.
— JEREMIAH 17:14 (NIV)

REFLECTION

- Are you carrying any thorns in your spirit or in your flesh?

- Are you struggling to work them out on your own? How is it going?

- Have you asked God for His grace and His help? Have you done so humbly and quietly?

- If you are still struggling alone, isn't it time to seek the comfort of the Holy Spirit?

Chapter 19

WASH ME; I AM DIRTY

If I told you that Reign loves to get a bath I would be lying. She adores water in any form (especially the water hose), but she hates soap. Giving her a bath is somewhere between steer roping and holding on to a greased pig. It is work!

Melisa and I use different methods. She tries to hold onto Reign's collar with one hand and wash her with the other, hence the "greased pig" metaphor. Melisa gets as wet and soapy as the dog, and I like to just stand back and watch, trying not to laugh too much.

My method is a little more direct. I leash her (Reign, not Melisa), pull her very close, and then stand on the leash while I wash her with two now-free hands. She pulls and yanks so hard sometimes that my feet almost come out from under me, but I haven't gone down yet. It is a battle, but it gets the job done.

Like Reign, we all need a bath from time to time, not just physically, but also emotionally and spiritually. We get dirty inside and out. True cleansing must take place in both our bodies and our minds.

The thing about taking a bath is that it requires preparation, effort, and action. It does not just happen. Taking a shower and getting clean on the outside is a habit that most of us think very little about; we just do it. Getting clean on the inside, however, is something that so many of us think very little about, and yet it just might be more important.

Daily, we invite the world to dump its garbage into our minds and our souls through the media, especially the constant barrage of news (again, mostly bad) on television and radio. Then there are the popular shows that denigrate the family while playing up the very worst of behaviors and portraying many degenerate aspects of our society as normal. With all of this, you have the recipe for a perfect storm of spiritual chaos. The world's dirt gets embedded in the pores of our minds, and unless cleansed, it calluses our hearts.

The Bible offers many examples of time spent in spiritual cleansing. Most notable is Jesus Christ's exodus into the desert for forty days to prepare His spirit and His body for the challenges and the work set before Him. He knew that to be His best, He needed to cleanse His spirit and quiet the clutter of the world. In essence, He took a forty-day-long spiritual bath.

Have you ever taken a spiritual bath? Have you looked around your home and taken note of the things you watch on television, listen to, or read? I encourage you to do that now. While doing it, ask yourself this question: "Is this something that makes me cleaner or dirtier in my spirit?" Self-examination is really not that hard, but it can be uncomfortable.

Shining a spotlight on the habits you routinely do or allow, though you know they are spiritually dirty, is the first step. After that, praying for help to replace these things with positive and uplifting choices brings clarity and guidance. The Apostle Paul gave us the roadmap in Philippians 4:8-9 (NIV) when he said:

> "Finally, brothers and sisters, whatever is true, whatever is noble, whatever is right, whatever is pure, whatever is lovely, whatever is admirable — if anything is excellent or praiseworthy — think about such things. Whatever you have learned or received or heard from me, or seen in me — put it into practice. And the God of peace will be with you."

Old habits rarely go away unless you replace them with new choices. For example, you could watch or read something uplifting, take a walk, or start an exercise program in place of watching the news or binge eating. Getting started, taking action, praying, and believing that you can do all things through Him who gives you power will build the consistency needed to break the chains of those destructive choices.

Old habits rarely go away unless you replace them with new choices.

The reality is that we will fall backwards from time to time. We are all human, and we will make mistakes. This why we need to routinely do spiritual and emotional cleansing, just like bathing and brushing our teeth. The world does not let up with the onslaught of garbage.

So, I told you that Reign hates getting a bath — but the interesting thing is that once the struggle is over, she prances around joyfully and gives us extra affection. We give her special privileges when she is clean. We allow her onto the sofa to sit between us, and we wrestle with her on the floor, among other things, all because the smell and the dirt once covering her is now gone. The truth is that once she is clean, we are able to give her greater and even more special blessing above what is needed.

Reign loves being clean; she just hates getting clean.

Our heavenly Father has greater blessing for us, too, and the only barrier to that is the dirt and filth we have allowed the world to pour over us. A spiritual "shower" may be the only thing needed to open the vaults of Heaven into your life and draw you closer to the Master.

Purge me with hyssop, and I shall be clean: wash me, and I shall be whiter than snow.

— PSALM 51:7 (KJV)

If we confess our sins, He is faithful and just to forgive us our sins, and to cleanse us from all unrighteousness.

— 1 JOHN 1:9 (KJV)

REFLECTION

- Are you inviting garbage into your life daily?

- Are there things you watch or read that you would be uncomfortable sharing with a small child or your grandmother?

- Do you sometimes just feel stressed out for no real reason? It may be time for an emotional input inventory. It also may be time to consider different choices. What have you got to lose?

IF I LAY ON HIS FEET, HE CAN'T LEAVE

Chapter 20

PLAYING IN THE WATER

Earlier, I mentioned that Reign adores water. That is a real understatement. When she is out, it is nearly impossible to do anything that involves a water hose. It seems her chief goal is to steal the hose and then prance about with it as she soaks everything in her path. The fact is, if she has the water, you are going to get wet.

One day I was out watering the plants in the back and had laid the running hose on the ground at the edge of a flower bed to give it a much-needed drink. I turned my back for just a moment and that was all Reign needed. She quickly picked the hose up by the end and began her water dance.

As I was chasing her around trying to get the hose without getting wet (which I failed at, by the way), Melisa came outside to see what was causing all the ruckus. Before I could warn her, Reign bolted toward her to show off the new prize. You have probably guessed it—Melisa and I both got soaked.

Reign's joy is almost magical to watch. It is as if all around her ceases in the presence of a stream of water. It is all she wants, and she will do all she can to get it.

The Word gives us so many examples that involve water. Most notable are the words of Jesus: "If anyone thirsts, let him come to Me and drink. Whoever believes in [trusts in, relies upon, obeys] Me, as the Scripture has said, out of their heart will flow rivers of living water" (John 7:37-38, NKJV).

> So many around us are thirsty for a drink of "living water," water that will wash away the anxiety, stress, and worry that seem to have engulfed our culture and lives.

So many around us are thirsty for a drink of "living water," water that will wash away the anxiety, stress, and worry that seem to have engulfed our culture and lives. The world offers mostly chaos and uncertainty to those who rely on it. It gives problems that parch our souls, and no solutions to quench our thirst. This is the plan of the enemy, to fill our minds with doubt, confusion and fear. Sadly, many seem to cling to these like a narcotic.

Jesus had a wonderful conversation with a Samaritan woman tending a well in John 4. I encourage you to take a moment and read the entire chapter; it is truly uplifting and enlightening. The high point is when Jesus tells her, "Everyone who drinks of this water [the water of the world] will be thirsty again, but whoever drinks of the water that I will give will never be thirsty again. The water that I will give him will become a spring of water welling up to eternal life." The woman said to him, "Sir, give me this water, so that I will not be thirsty or have to come here to draw water" (John 4:13–15, ESV).

The woman obviously didn't quite understand that Jesus was not talking about the water that the world can give from a common well; He was talking about the spiritual, living water. His is the only water that can clear the mind, bring peace to the soul, and reveal a joy that can weather any storm. This is just the tip of the iceberg that one can expect when they drink fully the "living water" offered freely by our Heavenly Father through Christ.

As believers, we are called specifically to demonstrate the effects of this in the manner in which we live and deal with those around us, especially those who have not yet found their way to the water. Out of our hearts are to "flow rivers of living water." We are to bathe those who meet with our joy, peace, and faith in the true reality, which is much greater than the world we see around us. We do this simply by refusing to buy into the lies of the enemy and trusting in our Father, no matter what is going on around us.

You are called by the Creator of all you see and perceive to be "light and salt" in a dark and tasteless land. You are called to guard your body, mind, and spirit from the lies that are set forth as truth by an enemy who wants nothing less than your destruction. You are called to be a witness in this parched and dry land to the thirst-quenching power of the "living water" that flows in your heart.

You are more than worthy with Him in your heart, and coursing through you now is the blood He shed for you.

I had the same questions you may have right now. "Who am I to share this living water? Have you any idea what I have done in my life? How can I possible represent the Lord of all creation? Nobody will listen to me." The truth is that you are not capable or really even worthy to do any of it on your own.

Here is the fantastic reality for those who have been called to follow Christ and serve the living God. You are more than worthy with Him in your heart, and coursing through you now is the blood He shed for you. You stand righteous (Romans 3:22), you are a joint heir to the power of Heaven (Romans 8:16–18), you have power over anything the enemy can throw at you (Luke 10:18–20), and you need not ever worry about what to say. When the time comes, the Father will give you the right words (Luke 12:12). Righteous, powerful, conquering, and eloquent is what you are when you bathe yourself in the "living water." Believe it and receive it, and it will make you into a person that shines with the light of eternal hope for everyone you meet.

When I see Reign dancing around with the water hose in her mouth, I think I see a glimpse of the image God wishes to see in us. She has total faith that we will care for her; she is completely reliant on us; and she demonstrates her love for us almost constantly. At the very same time, she wants to soak everything (and everyone) around her with those very things. She wants us all to be bathed in her joy and excitement. I think we are called to a similar path as we make our pilgrimage through this world to Heaven.

As the deer pants for streams of water, so
my soul pants for you, my God.
— PSALM 42:1 NIV

With joy you will draw water from the wells of salvation.
— ISAIAH 12:3 ESV

REFLECTION

- Are you feeling a little parched and thirsty for some good news?

- Is this world leaving you feeling confused and anxious sometimes? Do you see these qualities in those around you at home, at work, and in general?

- Are you ready to take a drink from the well of living water? The invitation is there. The cost has been paid, and the well never runs dry. Are you ready for joy and peace unlike anything you have ever known?

CELEBRATION

NO STICK IS TOO BIG

Chapter 21

RETURN HOME

One of the things I find so fascinating about dogs in general is the seemingly singular way they process time. It does not matter if their master is gone ten minutes or ten days; the greeting is the same. In Reign's case, it is a little obnoxious. I do have to confess; her excitement seems to be slightly magnified when I leave for an extended amount of time.

Recently, while I was on a two-week business trip, I would get daily updates from Melisa on Reign's mental state. I know it sounds a tad weird, but she is, after all, our "dog daughter." According to Melisa's reports, for the first few days, Reign would barely come out from under my desk. When she did, she would try to get into the dirty clothes — looking, I assume, for a pair of smelly socks.

As time marched on, I was told she grew more playful, but not back to 100 percent at all. That changed 1000 percent when I finally got back home. To say she was excited just does not quite do justice to the insanity of joy this pup demonstrated. Jumps, licks, hugs, moans, groans, excitement tinkles, and of course, she could not wait for me to get my socks off.

Fact is, any separation from either of us is too long for her. It is as if there is some void that only we can fill in her life. This is very evident when we take a trip and have someone come over and house sit for us. Reign is in her own house, her yard, getting everything she needs from someone else in terms of food and water. You would think that would suffice, and she would be content. But the young lady who watches Reign invariably tells us, "She laid about not really wanting to play; she hid in the closets and under furniture and does not seem to care about eating. I just couldn't seem to find any way to make her happy."

Reign's behavior demonstrates how I feel when I stray from the presence of my Heavenly Father. Notice I said, "when *I* stray." This is important to understand. God never leaves us. As a matter of fact, that is a promise He makes throughout the Word, in countless verses. The most well-known may be when Jesus gave the Apostles the "Great Commission" and reminded them, "I am with you always, to the end of the age" (Matthew 28:20, ESV).

The bottom line is that God is with the believer at all times. He never leaves, and He never strays. That being said, we can definitely stray.

"Always" is defined as, "perpetually, … without exception and on every occasion."[10] The bottom line is that God is with the believer at all times. He never leaves, and He never strays. That being said, we can definitely stray. I know this sounds contradictory. If God never leaves us, how can we leave Him?

The best illustration of how this is possible is Jesus' story about the prodigal son (Luke 15:11–32). The son in the story decided he'd had enough of his father's rules and decided to take off on his own. He left the safety and security of the house, took the blessings his father gave him, and chose to pursue the pleasures of the world. But though he left his father, his father never left him. The father's love, riches, and faith remained in place though the son did not.

We often make the same decision to take a "vacation" from God—to see what the world has to offer and have a little "fun." We stray away from the care and guidance so richly promised in the Holy Spirit. The truth is that initially, it may seem like we are suddenly free of the rules and able to do what we want, when we want. However, this is just a trap laid by an enemy that hates us, to drive a wedge between what we are and what we can be. This thinking eventually robs us of freedom while creating stress, anxiety, and guilt we can mask but never overcome on our own.

The prodigal son came to this realization after all his blessings seemed spent, and he found himself in the filth of a pigpen, eating what was meant for the swine. He understood that there was no way he could save himself from the mess he had made. He realized that only by returning to his father could he ever hope to be happy once again. So, he went back.

Interestingly, when he returned home, his father was not angry that he had squandered the blessings bestowed; he knew there were plenty more where they came from. He was not disappointed that his son had pursued the evil and sin of the world during his "vacation." The past was the past and not worth recounting. The father was also not repulsed by the stench and filth the son had covered himself with; he knew that was easily cleansed and washed away. There was nothing the son could do that the father could not forgive, cleanse, and make whole again. Nothing. You see, it was the son that strayed. The father's love and abundant blessing never left the son; it was always there, waiting to be lavished.

> *The father's love and abundant blessing never left the son; it was always there, waiting to be lavished.*

The Creator of all and the God of Heaven is no different from the father in this story. He never leaves us; He never takes away His promises, and His riches never diminish. He loves us so much that He is willing to watch us leave, be hurt, and even be crushed by the world only to find ourselves in total desperation. This is what it takes for so many to realize, believe, and accept that we can never be truly joyful, content, and blessed apart from Him.

Reign reminds me of this every time we return home. She demonstrates that even for a short time, she is not complete without us. Even though her physical needs are being met, there is a hole in her heart that only we can fill.

She has an immovable love for us and no matter how long we are gone, she accepts us again. She is not hurt or pouty; she shows only joy at our return. She embraces us with no reservation and with no conditions.

Therefore the LORD waits to be gracious to you, and therefore He exalts Himself to show mercy to you. For the LORD is a God of justice; blessed are all those who wait for Him.

— ISAIAH 30:18 (ESV)

Rejoice in the Lord always. Again, I will say, Rejoice!
— PHILIPPIANS 4:4 (NKJV)

REFLECTION

- Are you wandering about this world feeling lost and out of place?

- Are your physical needs being met, yet there is some vacuum that just cannot be filled by the world?

- Do you sometimes look in the mirror and feel repulsed by the filth you have allowed to cover you?

- Are you looking for greater peace and joy? Maybe it is time to return to the Father so that He may show you the place and purpose He has waiting for you.

NIGHT TIME CHILLIN'

Chapter 22

GROANINGS

Probably one of the most interesting things Reign does when either of us return home from any kind of outing is her groaning. Whether she greets us in the yard, by the car, on the porch, or in the house, it is the same. She whines and cries, and if we pet her at all, she has this deep, seemingly sorrowful, groan. I say "sorrowful" because I sometimes think it is her way of asking us to never leave again. She is at least telling us she suffered while we were gone, and her suffering does not end the instant we come home. She does not just forget about it. She has to work through it with us to feel better, though we might never really get what she is trying to tell us.

She groans from deep in her heart, and it always touches us and causes us to sneak her an extra treat. I think in her own way she knows what she feels; she is just unsure how to express it. What we do know is that her groanings are created out of love and likely reflect something that is beyond our understanding. We humans don't know exactly what she feels as a dog.

Sometimes when it comes to our spiritual lives, we can have a part that is just like Reign, feeling an inner "groaning," and another part that is not exactly able to figure out what it means. We just know we feel something. But it doesn't feel "simple." Have you ever wanted to say something or pray something, but you just could not figure out the words to use? For me, sometimes the emotion is so deep, the feelings so intense, that absolutely nothing I can come up with does it justice.

For example, if my beautiful wife, Melisa, were to look at me with those big brown eyes and ask, "Do you love me?", there is no way that simply saying "yes" could ever come close to how I feel about my love for her.

This is especially true when I am praying and is magnified when the prayer is in gratitude for all the blessings God has bestowed on me. No words can complete the humility, the mourning, and the joy I feel, all at once. It is not a simple feeling. Humility and mourning are present because I am well aware of my shortcomings, and yet I also have joy that these are cast as far as the east is from the west by His grace and His sacrifice. It is a cliché, but "Words truly can't do it justice."

So, what do we do? If there is no way we can ever adequately express our feelings toward God, what is the point? How can He ever know just how grateful we are and how much we love Him?

The wonderful thing about our Father is that He knew before time began that we would struggle with this, and He knew we would need divine help to communicate completely with Him. So, He gave us three very distinct things.

The first is His Word and promise found in the pages of the Holy Bible. Those who will read these words in faith and humility will get a glimpse into the very mind of God. Second, He came into the world as Christ so that we might be able to see how He intended man to behave and to show us the power of true faith in the eternal. Lastly, when Christ ascended to Heaven, He left us with the Holy Spirit so the minds of the faithful might be able to grasp the eternal truths in the Word.

> *When Christ ascended to Heaven, He left us with the Holy Spirit so the minds of the faithful might be able to grasp the eternal truths in the Word.*

The Father understood that in our fallen nature, when we are apart from Him, it is impossible for us to comprehend the vastness of what we have been given or to understand the true promise we have been offered. Our falling was not what He had intended, and we created it by our choices to sin and separate ourselves. This is where His love and grace are so evident. His desire to have a relationship with His most special creation—us—meant we needed help. In infinite love, He provided that help.

It is my belief that the Father, manifested as Jesus Christ, came so we might know and see the power intended for us at Creation. In doing so, He also gave us a path back to our original place as joint heirs to Heaven in eternity. The price He paid was enormous; the gift He gave us by sacrifice is incomprehensible to our minds. Christ even said to the disciples, "I have many things to say to you, but you cannot bear them now" (John 16:12). He left the Holy Spirit with us so that we might somehow gain a glimpse into the rest.

This Holy Spirit has been called many things. My favorite names for it are the Comforter, Wisdom, Understanding, Truth, and the Advocate. For me, these seem to sum up its nature nicely.

I think of a "comforter" as someone who aches with another who has had a misfortune. It is a person who reduces the negative intensity of an emotion, like fear, anger, guilt, or loss. The Holy Spirit has come to aid you in all that and more, if you will simply and faithfully ask. The comfort is there waiting for you, and all you have to do is take action.

Wisdom is a combination of experience, knowledge, and judgement crafted over time. There is no thing or being that is older or more knowledgeable and experienced than the Holy Spirit of the Creator of the universe. James tells us, "If any of you lacks wisdom, you should ask God, who gives generously to all without finding fault, and it will be given to you" (James 1:5, NIV).

"Truth. What is truth?"

Understanding and Truth go hand in hand because there can be no real understanding apart from truth. Pilate asked a great question of Christ when he said, "Truth. What is truth?" The interesting thing this is that Christ did not answer even though He knew. The premise of the question presupposed that Pilate did not possess the understanding to accept the truth. Many find themselves in that place because, while they may want the truth, they have not asked faithfully for wisdom to gain understanding, or they have created a "personal truth" for themselves that is completely outside the eternal reality. This is the apex of confusion for so many in our world today.

Advocate is my favorite name for the Holy Spirit, and it is the one that brings me the most peace. An advocate is defined as someone "who pleads for or on behalf of a person, cause, or idea."[11] The Holy Spirit physically takes your requests, your pain, your prayers, and your holy desires to the very throne of God to plead for you, not in finite human words but in the deep, spiritual groanings that surpass language and enter into the supernatural realm of Heaven. Do not worry about your words to God; just say them, and the Holy Spirit will do the rest. It is a promise that we can rely on no matter what.

Our Father has always known what we needed, He has always provided for us a way to Him personally, and He has paid all the costs to make sure we have access to it. This is the comfort of truth and the way to both wisdom and understanding. Your Advocate stands ready and simply waits for you take a step toward Him.

I do not see Reign ever ceasing with the groanings when we come back home; it is just a part of who she is inside. It is something I have grown to love, and knowing she loves me so much makes me feel special.

Likewise, I never can believe that the Holy Spirit will cease taking my prayers to God, using utterances and groanings that I cannot comprehend; it is just how things were designed. You are special, and God wants to hear from you. The words are not as important as the condition of your spirit toward Him.

Likewise the Spirit helps us in our weakness.
For we do not know what to pray for as we ought,
but the Spirit Himself intercedes for us with
groanings too deep for words.

— ROMANS 8:26 (ESV)

When the Spirit of truth comes, He will guide you into all truth,
for He will not speak on His own authority, but whatever
He hears He will speak, and He will declare to you
the things that are to come. He will glorify Me,
for He will take what is Mine and declare it to you.

— JOHN 16:13–14 (ESV)

REFLECTION

- Are you feeling like you just do not know how to pray?

- Do the words get jumbled up in your mind?

- Is the feeling just too hard to justify with words?
  I welcome you into the family of the faithful, where the
  right words are sometimes impossible to find. Say it
  anyway — pray it anyway — believe it anyway — accept it
  anyway.

Chapter 23

LET'S PLAY

Rocks and balls and sticks; oh my! These are Reign's favorite toys, and she is forever sticking them in our faces, legs... or worse. When she is ready to play, she makes a strong case. Most of the time, as you have probably guessed, we give in.

In the house, she goes for the ball. She has a variety to choose from. Some squeak, and, thankfully, some don't. If we are sitting down, she will come and gently lay her head in our laps, ball in mouth, and look up at us with those golden-brown eyes in quiet anticipation. It is as if we can hear her thoughts out loud: "BALL, ball, let's play."

Outside, the same is repeated, mostly with either a stick or a rock. The dog loves rocks!

Watching her chase whatever we may throw brings us as much joy as it does her. Seeing her happy gives us a sense of peace that we are providing what she needs. Truthfully, she does not always bring it back, and sometimes she will run away with it. This makes it hard to throw it again, since it is impossible for us to give her what she does not bring back to us.

Did you know that our Father in Heaven wants us to have fun? Numerous verses about celebration and abundant living appear throughout the Bible. The first recorded miracle performed by Jesus Christ happened at a wedding reception (which is a party) where He turned six jars of water (holding twenty to thirty gallons each) into wine. The wine was so good that the host of the party commented that it was the very best wine that had been served (John 2:1–11).

Make no mistake: Our Lord wants us to enjoy ourselves and live abundant lives while we are journeying through this world back to our true home. He only asks that we observe a few guidelines that, if you really consider them, are not heavy or restrictive; they are, in fact, light and freeing. Here is my take on three things I find in the Bible when it comes to having fun.

First, let's address the eight-hundred-pound gorilla: alcohol. In all honesty, I find nothing in the Word that says, "Do not drink alcohol." I do find many verses that warn of excessive drinking and being a "drunkard." Paul warned us that "drunkards… shall not inherit the kingdom of God" (Corinthians 6:10). That is a pretty strong warning for the believer and should not be dismissed.

My personal view is this: It seems to be okay to have a glass of wine with dinner. The warning comes in when one glass turns into a bottle (or two) and an evening state of drunkenness becomes normal. Proverbs 20:1 (KJV) tells us, "Wine is a mocker, strong drink is raging, and whosoever is deceived thereby is not wise." If you are going to have a drink, be wise, and do not be mocked by your own decisions.

Second, and I am going to quote the Apostle Paul here, because no one sums up our responsibility to our brothers and sisters in Christ better: "For the kingdom of God is not a matter of eating and drinking but of righteousness and peace and joy in the Holy Spirit. Whoever thus serves Christ is acceptable to God and approved by men. So then let us pursue what makes for peace and for mutual upbuilding. Do not, for the sake of food [or drink], destroy the work of God. Everything is indeed clean, but it is wrong for anyone to make another stumble by what he eats [or drinks]. It is good not to eat meat or drink wine or do anything that causes your brother [or sister] to stumble" (Romans 14: 17–21, ESV).

The bottom line here is that if you knowingly eat or drink something in front of someone who is either struggling with an issue or may find it spiritually confusing, then you are willfully causing them to potentially stumble in their walk of faith. This is a serious and ordained duty of all believers to be mindful of others. Just because you are strong in faith that does not mean the person sitting across the table is, and this must always be a consideration.

An example of this could be that you are at dinner with a group of friends and you know that someone at the table has been struggling with poor health due to overeating. If you order the largest, unhealthiest menu item and then follow it up with a big ice-cream dessert, you are creating a situation where the person could stumble back into what is making them sick. Remember, "do not, for the sake of food, destroy the work of God."

The same applies to having a drink with others. If you know that someone at the table is either struggling with addiction or may be offended by having alcohol on the table, you have the duty to abstain so your witness might not be tarnished and they might not stumble. Paul said in Romans 14:14 (NKJV), "I know and am convinced by the Lord Jesus that there is nothing unclean of itself, but to him who considers anything to be unclean, to him it is unclean." Our sacred call as believers is to be positive and uplifting examples to the world, and especially to fellow believers in Christ. In this, there is no wiggle room.

Lastly, Jesus Christ said, "I am come that they may have life, and that they might have it more abundantly" (John 10:10). "Abundance" is defined as "ample quantity," or "profusion."[12] In essence, to me it means unlimited and free. Jesus came that we might experience an unlimited life, but life without limits holds the possibility of both great pleasure and blessing along with great pain and self-sabotage.

> *The price of a good decision is light and easy to pay, while the cost of a bad decision can be heavy and just may take a lifetime to overcome.*

The Apostle Paul said, "All things are lawful for me, but not all things are helpful. All things are lawful for me, but I will not be dominated by anything." (1 Corinthians 6:12 ESV) Here is the crux of the matter: Jesus came to free believers in Him from the Old Testament Law, but He did not free us from the consequences of our taking excessive liberty with that freedom. The price of a good decision is light and easy to pay, while the cost of a bad decision can be heavy and just may take a lifetime to overcome.

God wants us to enjoy the life that He breathed into us. Jesus came that we might know and experience the unlimited abundance that has been here since the dawn of creation. How we exercise this liberty in Christ is our responsibility, and by our choices we will either enjoy the small price paid for good decisions or carry the large burden of cost for bad ones.

So, what about Reign? She takes her rock, ball, or stick and runs away with it, drops it, and doesn't bring it back. It is her choice, and when she does it, all the fun ends because I am not going to go get whatever it was and reinforce to her that we will bail her out of a bad decision. If we do, she just won't learn. It will get worse, and we will be chasing the ball with her.

Instead, we sit, wait, and watch as eventually she realizes that to get what she really wants, she must come back to us. The real fun, the true joy, comes from returning what we gave her. She knows and expects that when she comes back, we will reward her.

Our Father loves watching you have fun, and He wants to bless you more and more. He only requires that you be responsible with the liberty He has given by the sacrifice of Christ. He calls you to seek His guidance in all things and guard your brothers and sisters in the faith from stumbling into sin. He will not fail to keep His promises and to increase your joy and blessing as long as you turn and return to Him daily.

> *Our Father loves watching you have fun, and He wants to bless you more and more.*

You turned my wailing into dancing; you removed my sackcloth and clothed me with joy, that my heart may sing your praises and not be silent. LORD my God, I will praise you forever.

— PSALM 30:11-12 (NIV)

"Let Israel rejoice in their Maker; let the people of Zion be glad in their King. Let them praise His name with dancing and make music to Him with timbrel and harp."

— PSALM 149:2-3 (NIV)

REFLECTION

- Are you struggling with something that is causing you to stumble in your walk with God? Do you know someone who is?

- Does your behavior reinforce to others that you are a child of the Creator of the universe?

- Is there some burden you need to give back to God so He can bless you in a greater way? God sits patiently and watches, waiting for your return so that He may bless you abundantly, joyfully, and eternally. As always, the first step is yours to take.

Chapter 24

BUNNIES, BIRDS, AND LIZARDS—
"OH MY!"

"Wildlife beware: Reign is on the prowl. If you enter, you shall be chased." We should have this sign posted as a warning to anything that may dare to venture into our yard. She relishes the chase, and she will chase pretty much anything she sees.

I should note that Reign has never really caught anything. She just loves to stalk and pursue pretty much anything. The funniest thing to watch is her going after the birds. At our farm, we have an abundance of turkey vultures. These large, graceful flyers have a face that only a mother could love. They are, in short, very ugly.

I don't know that their general appearance matters much to Reign, but she cannot stand for them to be in the yard. At times, when a dozen or more have gathered by the pond, she will cry at the door until we release her to wreak havoc on them. Which, by the way, she really doesn't do. As she charges them, they simply lift gracefully off the earth and proceed to soar in circles about ten feet above her head.

She runs in her own circles below them, chasing them in the air and barking, as if to say, "That's not fair! Get back down here so we can play!" Occasionally, one will swoop down within a couple of feet of her as if mocking her.

She doesn't understand that if she would just be still, lie down, and be quiet, they would likely come back to earth. They are clearly not afraid of her; she is just a bit too frenetic for them.

So often, we allow what we are chasing to blind us to what we really need to do to "catch it."

As I watch her, I am reminded that, so often, we allow what we are chasing to blind us to what we really need to do to "catch it." Our misplaced priorities and the world we have allowed to be created in our homes, our minds, and our workplaces create a frenzied routine that robs so many of opportunity and thus the ability to slow down and truly think. As Pogo once said, "We have met the enemy, and he is us."

When God created the world we live in, He granted Adam and Eve complete dominion over everything. He assured them they would want for nothing and would have peace and happiness as long as they placed their trust in Him. It was paradise... but they wanted more.

We all know the story—the serpent Satan, a garden, the apple, a few bites, and paradise was lost. It was a bad choice, and mankind has paid the price for millennia. The truth is that our modern world continues to make virtually the same bad choice every day. Our decision to put the pursuit of things that are temporary far ahead of the eternal simply compounds daily, adding to and increasing the effect of the original choice made in that garden.

The Creator's inspired Word gives us a simple, very clear way out: "Be still and know that I am God" (Psalm 46:10). This is about as simple as it gets. The challenge is that while it may be simple to grasp, it is not necessarily easy to do in the hectic and frenzied personal world we have created.

The basic truths of the Bible do not require divine revelation from the Holy Spirit. They do not even require the reader to be a believer. For instance, the Ten Commandments (Exodus 20:1–17), for the most part are pretty straightforward and really require no discernment or wisdom to grasp. As a matter of fact, most were the foundational elements for almost all of western civilization morals and laws for centuries.

Jesus told us, "Love your neighbor as yourself" (Mark 12:31, ESV). This is basically the Golden Rule, "Do unto others as you would have them do unto you." Whose grandmother did not preach this to them when they were young? Not complex stuff, and yet so many walk in a dazed, confused, and anxiety-ridden life because they have chosen frenzy over faith.

Everyone is searching for the things that are promised in the Bible — things like love, joy, peace, security, hope, and forgiveness. But they are searching in a world that will never give those to them. For many, it comes down to the fact that they want all the gifts of God, just without God. The cliché, "Know God, Know Peace. No God, No Peace," has never been truer than it is for the modern man and woman.

> For many, it comes down to the fact that they want all the gifts of God, just without God.

Do not misunderstand me: The deeper truths of the Bible do require the Holy Spirit to open the eyes of the mind and heart in order for us to understand and discern them. However, this cannot truly happen until we exercise the simplest of the Father's requests, "Be still and know that I am God." Quiet, belief, and faith all precede revelation. Then, like a summer rain, will God pour over your life peace, joy, and blessing.

At the end of this chapter are two verses that spell out what the enemy has stolen from us and how we can get it back. Again, it is not hard to understand, but it does take action, and that action begins with you. "The effectual fervent prayer of a righteous man [or woman] availeth [accomplishes] much" (James 5:16, KJV).

I challenge you right here, right now. Start today: Look at the pace of your life and pick one single thing that you can eliminate and replace with rest, quiet, and being still. Maybe it is a club you have joined, one of your children's multiple activities, or a habit that, if you are honest with yourself, is just something to kill time.

Time killers can be spirit crushers if they are not minded. Give it some thought and ask yourself, "What have I got to lose?" More importantly, "What do I stand to gain?" Good questions.

So, back to Reign. She likely won't get that her chase is fruitless. She's a puppy. God hardwired it into her, and it is unlikely she will stop, at least not until she gets older and tired of being frustrated.

Doesn't that sound familiar? There comes a time when we all get tired of it, and for some, that time comes too late. My prayer for you is that today is a line of demarcation. Today is the day you decide to "be still."

And God blessed them. And God said to them, "Be fruitful and multiply and fill the earth and subdue it, and have dominion over the fish of the sea and over the birds of the heavens and over every living thing that moves on the earth."

— GENESIS 1:28 (ESV)

If My people, who are called by My name, shall humble themselves, and pray, and seek My face, and turn from their wicked ways; then will I hear from heaven, and will forgive their sin and will heal their land.

— 2 CHRONICLES 7:14 (KJV)

REFLECTION

- What non-productive time killers could be eliminated from your life? When asking yourself this question, are you being honest?

- Do you feel stressed, anxious, and overwhelmed by the pace of your day and your life? Go back to the first question. What killers can you eliminate so that you can find a few moments to "be still"?

REST

NINE BALL IN THE SIDE POCKET

Chapter 25

UNDER OUR FEET

My wife is an excellent cook, and when I say this, I mean "five-star" great. She has also become a bit of a cooking contortionist as she maneuvers the kitchen obstacle course that is Reign.

Not too long ago, Melisa was preparing her world famous (at least in my world) fried chicken, greens, and cauliflower mashed potatoes. As she pulled the chicken out and turned to set it on the kitchen island behind her, I witnessed an acrobatic feat unlike any I had ever seen. While Melisa was at the stove, Reign had stealthily positioned herself right behind her and laid down.

As Melisa placed the chicken on the plate and turned, Reign jumped up simultaneously—because her favorite treat is, of course, chicken jerky. My wife stumbled, the dog went between her legs, twice! I saw it all and thought only a master class in juggling and gymnastics would save dinner.

My wife dipped and jumped, the dog weaved and dodged — but nothing hit the ground. Dinner was safe, and despite causing near disaster, Reign got a few bites. Moral of the story: The dog is always in our way!

Earlier I told you how Reign would lie at my feet under my desk as I worked, and how endearing it was to see her desire just to be close and feel safe. What I did not tell you is that she is almost constantly underfoot at pretty much any other time too.

Besides the kitchen, Reign is literally 100 percent at our feet, in our path, or trying to get there. When we are walking through the house, she is right beside us, and if we go outside for a walk, she makes a habit to repeatedly cut in front of us and at some points just stop at our feet, as if to say, "See, I am still here." Yes, it is obnoxious and a tad annoying. It has almost caused me to take a tumble on occasion, but you can bet we are always aware that she is there and have no doubt that she loves us.

When Reign forces her presence on us, in some cases we push her away, but most of the time we just stop, give her a little love and she gives us a break. Her unrelenting persistence for our attention usually pays off in her favor. She knows it and expects it.

In Luke 18:1-8, Jesus tells us about a persistent widow who epitomizes the old saying, "the squeaky wheel gets the grease." This lady needed the help of a judge, but he would not listen to her plea "for a while." We are led to believe that during this time she would not relent; she pursued the judge and forced her way into his awareness repeatedly. Finally, the judge gave in and granted her desire. He made the decision to hear her case because, to para- phrase his words, "This widow will not leave me alone, and if I don't give her what she wants, she will just keep coming and coming until she wears me out."

In the Sermon on the Mount Matthew 7:9–11 (NKJV), Christ challenged the depth of the listeners' trust when He said, "Or what man is there among you who, if his son asks for bread, will give him a stone? Or if he asks for a fish, will he give him a serpent? If you then, being evil, know how to give good gifts to your children, how much more will your Father who is in Heaven give good things to those who ask Him!" What loving parent would not bless their child when they had the chance? There is no parent with a greater love for His children than our Father in Heaven.

I believe the lesson in these two passages is that we are called to persistently pray in faith, believing we will be blessed and trusting that God's response will be what we need. This does not mean we will always get what we want; however, it does mean we will always get what is best for us. In a popular song, we are reminded that some of God's most powerful blessings come in the form of what some might think of as unanswered prayers. Looking back on my life, I can give testimony to that fact, time and time again.

> Some of God's most powerful blessings come in the form of what some might think of as unanswered prayers.

In raising our two children, we blessed them and gave them what they needed, but they absolutely did not always get what they wanted. For a child, this is often confusing and upsetting, and you may hear something like, "If you loved me, you would give this to me." Yet, it was because you love them that they did not get their wish. This is something loving parents understand, but children often do not until they have a family of their own.

As my children have become increasingly independent, I have offered advice based on mistakes I made and they ignored it and in essence made the same bad decision, and I have seen the pain that their choice caused. It is hard to watch. However, we humans are stubborn, and quite often, failure is the best teacher.

This is where so many find a stumbling block in their relationship with the Lord. They just can't understand why God would allow such pain into their lives. They don't realize they're the ones bringing the pain in. The answer usually lies within the choices they made over time that led up to their predicament. When we rely solely on our own understanding, we will often find ourselves in perilous situations of our own making.

There is a better way, and once again it is simple and carries with it a promise from God. Proverbs 3:5-6 (NIV) tells us, "Trust in the LORD with all your heart, and lean not on your own understanding; in all your ways submit to Him and He will make your paths straight." He says, "will," not "might," or "maybe will." The statement is definitive. Trust the Father completely. Forget your own childish thinking, accept completely who He is, and grace will compel Him to fulfill His promise to direct your path in the way that you should go.

This is power. This is a promise. This is exactly what God wants you to expect when your belief, faith, and trust are in Him. You have the ultimate Counselor in your corner, and no greater wisdom lies at your fingertips than what is within the pages of the Bible.

As I mentioned, we do not always give love exactly when Reign wants it. It is kind of tough when we are walking to the house with our arms full of groceries or when I am putting something together (like a grill) that requires my attention. We sometimes have to say no because the timing is just not right.

The Father is no different. His plan is not something we can understand. However, oftentimes He is just busy bringing in a blessing that we are not expecting, or He is putting something together that we cannot see that will bring us even greater abundance. We only need to trust Him.

By the way, the groceries we bring almost always contain some treat for Reign, and she has reaped great reward from the grill in terms of bones and leftovers. She just did not understand that while she may have felt pushed away, we were in fact making a way to bless her even more. Funny how that works.

Be anxious for nothing, but in everything
by prayer and supplication, with thanksgiving,
let your requests be made known to God.
— PHILIPPIANS 4:6 (NKJV)

And I tell you, ask, and it will be given to you; seek,
and you will find; knock, and it will be opened to you.
For everyone who asks receives, and the one who seeks
finds, and to the one who knocks, it will be opened.
— LUKE 11:9-10 (ESV)

REFLECTION

- Is there some way that you believe God has disappointed you?

- Have you talked about it with Him?

- Have you taken the time to read His Word, be quiet, and listen for His answer?

- Are you grateful now for some "unanswered prayers" from the past, once you realize the plan God had was so much better?

- Are you trusting God, leaning on Him for understanding, and then waiting for His direction? Maybe it is time.

Chapter 26

ON THE COUCH

Sitting on the couch and watching a movie or show is something Melisa and I enjoy doing together. We are both addicted to snack mixes, and so is Reign. Recently, while watching a rerun of the classic TV series, *MASH* (just like music, the best stuff is the old stuff), and getting settled in beside each other, the dog decided she was not content at our feet. She jumped up and forced her way in between us while Melisa and I juggled drinks and snack mix.

Melisa looked at the dog and exclaimed, "Careful, you are getting to be a big dog now!" Now firmly perched between us, Reign looked around as if thinking, "What dog?"

I am convinced that in some way Reign believes she is human, or at least a very close equivalent.

While we are watching anything, Reign perks her ears and continually cocks her head from side to side, studying what is happening on the screen. Occasionally, she will look at us, brighten her eyes, and give us a dog smile as if to say, "I think I am starting to get it. What do you think?" When she does things like that, we just can't resist giving her extra love and belly scratches.

Our relationship with God and His call on our lives is very similar. He desires that we draw close to Him and intently work toward greater understanding of His will and His Word. I believe God draws the greatest pleasure from a believer who will make it a priority to draw close to Him in bold, hope-filled prayers and study His Word with the single desire of understanding Him more.

If you have never read the book of Proverbs, I highly recommend that you do. I suggest you begin as soon as possible. The book is filled with guidance on navigating the spiritual minefield of this fallen world and those who inhabit it. It addresses nearly every life scenario, but the book's overriding theme is the direction to seek God's wisdom first. In fact, the book tells us that God's wisdom is the most valuable of all things.

Blessed is the one who finds wisdom, and the one who gets understanding, for the gain from her is better than gain from silver and her profit better than gold. She is more precious than jewels, and nothing you desire can compare with her. Long life is in her right hand; in her left hand are riches and honor. Her ways are ways of pleasantness, and all her paths are peace. She is a tree of life to those who lay hold of her; those who hold her fast are called blessed (Proverbs 3:13–18 ESV).

These powerful words carry a mighty promise: that if you seek wisdom, you will gain greater understanding. All the rest will fall into place, and you will be blessed. Once again, we see that word "seek," which absolutely implies a required action. Seeking indicates a search for something that must be uncovered. If you were mining (searching) for actual silver and gold, you would require shovels, digging, and dedication to find the precious ore.

Seeking wisdom is really no different from mining, with the exception that the tool is the Word of God, the Bible. You will likely get a little dirty (maybe a lot) as the pages begin to reveal to you the sin that has stained your life. You will have to be dedicated to digging deeper, reading and re-reading some passages, chapters, and even whole books until the message begins to open up to you. This is not something you can do once a week for an hour. Can you imagine a gold miner showing up just one morning a week and digging for only an hour or two? We both know all he would do is scratch the surface of what was there.

If you feel that you are "digging deeper" and not finding what you need, you might need to check your tools.

If you feel that you are "digging deeper" and not finding what you need, you might need to check your tools. Many people do not mine in the Bible; they study and read books or guides that may quote a verse here and there but are filled with the author's opinions. There is nothing the matter with that — as a matter of fact, I am one of those writers. The reality is that a variety of true faith-based works is good, but if reading them takes the place of consistently reading the Bible, once again, you are just scratching the surface of what is available to you.

That is exactly why so many believers find themselves frustrated in their faith. They are only seeing the surface of the true glory of God. They do not realize that the digging requires consistent, daily communion with the Creator through prayer and study of His Word. Just as in any other relationship, we have to communicate. It is really a form of insanity to believe that another person would open up to us though we are not willing to talk to them. Our Father is no different.

The Holy Spirit cannot teach us and reveal the mysteries to us if we are not willing to do some digging. This requires that we set aside time at some point each day to study and be quiet in prayer. Remember: God does not compete for our time. He does not force His way into our minds, nor does He shout over the noise of our lives. Our job is to make our way to Him and shut out the world, if only for a time, so the Holy Spirit may softly speak to our hearts and souls.

Reign struggles and strives to understand us and the world of her home. She forces her way into our presence, she reclines beside us, she is quiet, and she listens. What an incredible snapshot of how I believe we are to behave as we seek a deeper relationship with our Father in Heaven. The more we come to Him, the more we submit ourselves, the more He promises to give us understanding and wisdom here, along with revelation of the place that is to be our eternal home.

> *But when He, the Spirit of truth, comes, He will guide*
> *you into all the truth. He will not speak on His own*
> *initiative, but whatever He hears He will speak, and He*
> *will declare to you the things that are to come.*
>
> — JOHN 16:13 (ESV)

If any of you lacks wisdom, let him ask God, who gives to all liberally and without reproach, and it will be given him. But let him ask in faith, with no doubting, for the one who doubts is like a wave of the sea that is driven and tossed by the wind.

— JAMES 1:5-6 (NKJV)

REFLECTION

- Do you need more wisdom and understanding to handle the challenges of this life?

- Are you digging for the answers or just scratching the surface?

- If you are digging and not finding what you need, are you using the right tools?

- Is it time to start a routine of daily mining in the Word? Remember, the treasure you seek is more valuable than silver, gold, and precious jewels. What are you waiting for?

BIG GIRL

Chapter 27

THE FOOT OF THE BED

Earlier, I shared with you that Reign is always at our feet each morning when we get up, full of energy and in total "licking and whining" mode. She is also at our feet every night when we go to bed, but with a little different attitude — she is quiet and looking for rest. The interesting thing is that she will not come into the bedroom until the last person makes it to bed. Most of the time, that last person is me.

Once we are snuggly under the covers, we can hear her lie down and give the last deep sigh of relief before she drifts off to sleep. I think she needs us all together so she can feel safe, relax, and reach a state where she can find rest and relief from the weariness of the day.

Rest is so critical to our ability to function to our highest potential, and we really can't be at our best without it. Yet so many people don't appreciate the value of a good night's sleep to revive the body.

They don't see the need to take a break from work at times just to relax and clear the mind. The trend in a lot of households is to stay up late watching TV, playing a video game, or working. If this becomes a long-term habit, the results can damage your mental health and your soul.

Now don't get me wrong here. I do not believe there is a problem with occasionally staying up to catch the end of a great movie or pulling a super-late night finishing a project. Just ask Melisa; she will tell you that when I am writing and in the zone, it is nothing for me to stay up well into the early morning hours. It is quiet; nothing else is going on, and I can buzz through several thousand words pretty quickly. However, the honest truth is that when I do this, my mind is in a bit of a fog for a couple of days afterwards.

The Bible contains many instructions regarding the importance of getting rest. One is a command to keep the Sabbath day holy. Why would honoring this day be a directive? The truth is that God knew we would all lead busy lives that would seem to require constant work, from the early days of farming the land to what we have now — a constant barrage from the world of gotta-get-it-done-now-itis. It is easy to think, "I just do not have time to rest today."

The reality is that we need rest, and we need a consistent day to do nothing as it relates to work. The old adage "All work and no play (or rest), makes Jack (and Jill) dull" has never been truer. The word "dull" is defined as lacking sharpness, losing an edge, lacking in brilliance or zest, sluggish, cloudy, and slow in perception.[13] This pretty accurately describes me after a writing all-nighter. I am sure you can relate to many of these qualities if you have stayed up too late and had to get up early the next day, or if you have worked many consecutive days with no day off. God knew we needed a break, and He instructed us to take it every week for our own good and to remember Him.

In many other places throughout the Word, our Father tells us the many benefits of rest, particularly the blessing we find when that rest includes Him. In the 23rd Psalm (NKJV), David writes, "He makes me to lie down in green pastures, He leads me beside the still waters. He refreshes my soul." Jesus said, "Come to me, all you who are weary and heavy laden, I will give you rest" (Matthew 11:28, NKJV). God understands that the burdens of this life can be heavy, and He offers refreshing and peaceful rest to those who desire it.

Desire it? We all want to be refreshed and rested, right? Of course we do. The challenge is finding rest in the chaos we tend to build in "our" world. The materialism that drives so many, combined with the battering of bad news and discontent

> The challenge is finding rest in the chaos we tend to build in "our" world.

from every outlet of the media, make finding rest very hard on our own. To remedy this problem, people often turn to things such as alcohol, sleep aids, or drugs. Here is an idea that has been around for a few millennia: turn to God and ask for His rest and refreshment. He promises to give it to those who seek Him and ask.

If you are having challenges with sleep and rest, give this a try.

Carve out fifteen quiet minutes every evening and read a chapter from the book of Psalms. With the exception of chapter 119, they are pretty short, and all will bring comfort to you.

When you finish, you will have time left, so say a prayer asking God to open your spirit to what you just read. The message may not be clear to you at first; that is okay and, honestly, normal. Ask for clarity. This is why He sent the Holy Spirit to us — so that we might be enlightened about what we may not understand at first.

End your prayer by giving thanks for at least one thing that happened to you during the day. Boldly claim that you will have a good night's rest and that you will wake up refreshed in the morning.

Lastly, fight all the doubt that the enemy will throw at you and believe, really believe, that rest is coming.

Do not give up after one night. Some mental clutter may take a few nights to clear out. God is faithful, but He does not compete, and the Holy Spirit is an excellent de-clutterer (is that a word?). You simply have to commit to being consistent for a time.

All that sounds simple and easy, right? It is, but I have to share this with you. What you do with the last hour of the night before your reading time will tremendously affect how quickly the last fifteen minutes will take hold. If you bombard your mind with negative news, violent movies, or video games, you will likely find it tough to give the material your full attention. Remember, the enemy of rest is chaos. Don't put yourself behind at the start by feeding that chaos late at night.

These words from Paul are the best closing argument I can find: "Do not be anxious about anything, but in every situation, by prayer and petition, with thanksgiving, present your requests to God. And the peace of God, which transcends all understanding, will guard your hearts and your minds in Christ Jesus" (Philippians 4:6-7, NIV). The formula is simple; the decision is yours.

When Reign comes into our room at night as we prepare for bed, I can imagine her thoughts by her actions. She stands beside us with her ears laid back in complete submission, and we give her love. She then perks up just a little and returns the love as if to say,

"Thank you for everything you did for me today." She then quietly lies down, and that is it—she is out.

(Small confession here: She sometimes takes a moment to search out a smelly pair of socks to sleep with, finding her usual comfort in being bathed in the aroma of her master. Is that not a lesson for us all? God bless you, and good night!)

> *I will both lie down in peace, and sleep; For You*
> *alone, O LORD, make me dwell in safety.*
> — PSALM 4:8 (NKJV)

> *Come to me, all you who are weary and burdened, and I will*
> *give you rest. Take My yoke upon you and learn from Me, for*
> *I am gentle and humble in heart, and you will find rest for*
> *your souls. For My yoke is easy and My burden is light.*
> — MATTHEW 11:28-30 (NIV)

REFLECTION

- Are you protecting your "off" time?

- Are you taking time every week to rest and refresh your body and soul?

- Is a good night's rest sometimes elusive?

- What is your nightly routine? How are you spending the last hour before bed? Reconsidering this time just might make all the difference in the world to you.

DID SOMEONE SAY BALL?

Chapter 28

SLEEPING AND DREAMING

Have you ever just sat and watched a dog that has finally drifted off into a deep sleep? Their legs move; they sometimes let out a low groan or cry and from time to time, a subtle "woof." I can imagine they are dreaming of something enjoyable, such as chasing another animal, eating a good meal, or getting love and attention. Many dogs don't visibly dream often, and it is really neat to watch.

Reign dreams; I am sure of it. I know she doesn't really understand this, but watching her dream, twitch, and groan gives us great joy. The joy comes from knowing that we have created for her a refuge where she can be completely vulnerable, with no fear.

This is a mirror of what God intends for those who will call upon His name and believe the promises given in His Word. He has created a peaceful, safe place for us to rest so that He may reveal His greatness and glory. All we need do is have faith, ask, and receive it into our hearts by way of our Savior Jesus Christ. The Father will handle the details if we will submit and let Him.

Sleeping comprises about one-third of our lives and dominates most of our time spent here on earth. In fact, you may have never even considered the true spiritual nature of sleep and God's intentions for it in our spiritual walk. Sleep is the gift of rest and refreshment. It is also a way that God gains glory as we close our eyes and drift off, completely exposed and trusting in His protection. We magnify God's glory when we are totally submissive and acknowledge our vulnerability.

Psalm 91 (NIV) has a few passages (verses 1, 5 and 11) about the comfort God provides to those who will trust in Him when they are most vulnerable. "Whoever dwells in the shelter of the Most High will rest in the shadow of the Almighty. You will not fear the terror of night, nor the arrow that flies by day... For He will command His angels concerning you to guard you in all your ways."

Our Father has committed, promised, and guaranteed His protection to those who seek it and trust Him. The one and only thing that I am absolutely certain of in this world is that God keeps His promises and never wavers in His commitments. The prophet Isaiah wrote, "O Lord, You are my God. I will exalt You. I will praise Your name, for You have done wonderful things, plans formed of old, faithful and sure" (Isaiah 25:1, ESV). One of His plans is for you to find comfort, rest, refuge, and sleep in the perfect shelter of His love. I know it because it is written in His holy and inspired Word, the Bible — his love letter to mankind, handed down over thousands of years, to generation after generation.

"For God so loved the world that He gave His only Son, that whoever believes in Him should not perish but have eternal life"

(John 3:16, NIV). It is my belief that this is the apex verse of the Bible and the cornerstone upon which those plans were "formed of old"—plans for you to be joyful, peaceful, and restful. This verse gives us three declarations of love and one single action step for us. God loved, He sacrificially gave, and He offers eternal life with Him. It is not complicated. All we are called to do is believe in His Word and then trust He is faithful in His promise.

Jesus Christ challenged us and made a promise when He said, "But seek ye first the kingdom of God... and all these things shall be added unto you" (Matthew 6:33, KJV). "All these things" are the commitments, promises, and guarantees laid out across the living pages of God's Word. Never doubt that the Creator of the universe loves you, has plans for your good, and faithfully wills to see them completed if you will seek Him.

So how do we get back to Reign and her twitching on the floor? Simple. She knows and accepts our love. She does not doubt that we have her best interests at our core, and she has complete faith that we will provide for and protect her. She is able to rest and dream because this knowledge gives her peace. She trusts us, blesses our lives, and as a result, we choose to bless her at every opportunity. In a snapshot, that is God's promise to us.

> *"For I know the plans I have for you," declares*
> *the LORD, "plans to prosper you and not to harm*
> *you, plans to give you hope and a future."*
> — JEREMIAH 29:11 (NIV)

And behold, I am with you always, even to the end of the age.
— MATTHEW 28:20 (ESV)

O soul are you weary and troubled?
No light in the darkness you see.
There's light for a look at the Savior, and
life more abundant and free.
Turn your eyes upon Jesus, look full in his wonderful face.
And the things of earth will grow strangely dim
In the light of his glory and grace.
— HELEN LEMMEL[14]

REFLECTION

- Have you given your trust to God?

- Are you looking for a true place of refuge and rest?

- Is this world giving you what you need to feel safe and protected?

- Do you seek eternal peace and confidence? Maybe it is time to turn your eyes and heart to the one who can provide the true peace that surpasses all understanding.

BREAK TIME BETWEEN CHASING SOCKS AND BALLS

EPILOGUE

THE ROAD LESS TRAVELED

To make a confession, I have never been a dog person, though we have had a few. My wife and my kids are a different story—they have loved them all like family.

Reign showed me a different path, and through her, I believe God has revealed much to me and about me. She gave me a great gift, and one that was totally unexpected: She caused me to draw closer than ever to the Creator and our Savior.

In 1915, Robert Frost wrote "The Road Not Taken." When I read it many decades ago, it had a tremendous impact that has lasted across the spectrum of my life. The last line of the poem reads, "Two roads diverged in the wood, and I—I took the one less traveled by, and that has made all the difference."[15] The lesson in those few words changed my life and truly "made all the difference."

Making a different choice than those around you can be difficult in any environment and can sometimes cause a division between you and people you considered friends, and even family. The decision to leave your secure job and start out in your own business, or to pick up roots, leave your home, and move across the country with your family to pursue an opportunity are examples of decisions that could create a rift with those you love. In many cases, they just do not understand the "still, small voice" that is whispering to *your* soul, and it is very likely that they never will.

The apostle Paul outlined just such a choice when he said, "Do not be conformed to this world, but be transformed by the renewing of your mind, that you may prove what is the good and acceptable and perfect will of God" (Romans 12:2, NKJV).

Jesus described the path when He said, "Enter through the narrow gate. For the wide is gate and broad is the road that leads to destruction, and many enter through it. But small is the gate and narrow the road that leads to life, and only a few find it" (Matthew 7:13–14, NIV).

I believe the theme of both of these verses is that to experience the fullness of God's promise—the true joys of this life—and to know His will for our lives, we must take the road less traveled. This literally means looking around at what the masses of people are doing, watching, and following, and then doing something completely different — in many cases, the exact opposite. Trust me: When you make this decision, most won't understand. Some will think you are crazy, and "friends" will show their true colors. It is actually a very cleansing exercise but can be emotionally painful. I believe this is what Jesus was referring to as the hard or constricting gate because by choosing that path, you will leave some people behind, by their choice.

Deciding to trust God, accepting Jesus Christ as Savior, and picking a new path may seem strange to those you currently hang out with, and they may even give you a hard time for choosing not to pursue the things of the past. Your sudden disdain for watching profanity-laced movies, your new habit of giving thanks before a meal or skipping the regular Friday night drinking party may cause them to criticize and make fun of you, or they may even look at your new choices as criticizing or judging of them. The latter is really interesting because I find that people who serve the world are often convicted by the mere presence of someone who serves the Lord without a word being spoken. This should not surprise you; actions do speak significantly louder than words.

While writing this devotional, I have come to realize more and more that when Jesus said. "Come to me, all you who are weary and burdened, and I will give you rest. Take my yoke upon you and learn from me, for I am gentle and humble in heart, and you will find rest for your souls. For my yoke is easy and my burden is light" (Matthew 11:28–30 NIV), He was, of course, right. It is in fact the yoke and the burden of this fallen world that is heavy and crushing.

This is no more evident than when a believer chooses to invoke God to make a stand for life, for balanced education, or for prayer in the public sector. It is not the weight of Christ that comes to bear; it is literally the weight of the world. This culture seems to be less and less open to anything that might shine a light on its failings and sin.

So, my prayer for you is that if you are a person of faith, somehow this book has made you a little stronger and given you renewed faith and trust while all the time drawing you closer to God. If you are looking to follow this with something, I would suggest the Book of Romans. Chapter one reads like today's headlines, and the chapters following contain the roadmap to living victoriously in Christ. Take your time reading it, though; there is a lot of power to unpack.

If you are a new believer, find a fellowship of like-minded people, devote yourself to talking to God every chance you get, and dig into His Word. Start with the Psalms; there you will find the love and heart of God. After that, turn to the New Testament. Ask in faith for the Holy Spirit to lead you where you should read next, and He will.

This is the road less traveled — the way, the truth, and the life. When the road diverges in the forest of confusion created by this world, ask God for guidance, be submissive to His leading, trust that He intends nothing but your good to happen, and then go wherever He leads. That has been my path for the past twenty years, and it has made all the difference for me. It can for you, too.

So, then faith comes by hearing, and hearing by the Word of God.
— ROMANS 10:17 (NKJV)

God bless you, and happy trails!

THANK YOU

"Thank you" is such a simple thing to say, and in so many instances, it pales in expressing true gratitude. That being said, I have to acknowledge a few people who helped me in getting these thoughts out of my ever-cluttered head and into print.

To my wife, Melisa, my "girlfriend" for nearly four decades, who did a masterful job selling me on getting another dog. I did not want the dog at the time, and now I can't imagine life without her.

To my family, who has supported me in nearly every endeavor over my lifetime, and especially to my parents, Libby and Melvin. The lessons they taught me about marriage and raising a family have led me to become the man I am today. Thank you, Mama and Daddy.

To my grandmother, Sara Sue, who is standing in Heaven looking down at me — and I felt her spirit throughout this project. She dragged me to church every time the lights were on, right up until I got married, and she made sure that I was "trained up in the way that I should go." Although I have for sure strayed, I have never departed that path. Thank you, Nanny.

To the team at Niche Pressworks, especially my editor, Melanie, who kept me focused (which is no small feat) and on target during this process. Their diligence and planning played a major role in producing the best possible end result. I am grateful we found each other.

Most importantly, I lift gratitude and praise to our Father in Heaven, our Savior that stands at His side, and the Holy Spirit dwelling in my heart. My prayer is that in some way, this book might reignite in others the peace, joy, and love for the Word that has been rekindled in my heart. Thank You, Lord, for the blessings of this journey, undeserved but not unappreciated.

For I am convinced that neither death nor life, neither angels nor demons, neither the present nor the future, nor any powers, neither height nor depth, nor anything else in all creation, will be able to separate us from the love of God.

— ROMANS 8:38–39 (NIV)

ABOUT THE AUTHOR

With more than thirty-five years of experience in the field of management and training, Bart Christian has built from scratch three business that have stood the test of time, the last twenty-five years being focused mainly within the K-12 school nutrition market.

Bart's southern style and subtle humor, combined with his hands-on experience, have made him a top-rated speaker and audience favorite from coast to coast, speaking on the topics of leadership, communication, customer service, sanitation, and food safety. After authoring the top-selling book series, *Simple Solutions*, which provides easy, step-by-step solutions to everyday people problems, Bart decided to turn his writing skills toward sharing his strong Christian faith with others of like minds and hearts. His love of and passion for scripture, as well as his gratitude toward God for his successes, are what led him to write this devotional book, *Eager for the Master.*

Bart and his wife (a.k.a. "girlfriend") of over 35 years, Melisa, live on their farm in Georgia with a beloved assortment of dogs, cats, chickens, and other (mostly wild) animals. Of course, no farm would be complete without a temperamental tractor, fences in a constant state of disrepair, and a garden that seems to grow weeds better than veggies. Bart commented that, "The farm life is work, and like life, it yields back what you put into it (or don't) — pressed down, shaken together, and overflowing."

SCHEDULE A SPEAKING ENGAGEMENT

To schedule Bart for speaking engagements, contact him at Bart@BartChristian.com.

STAY CONNECTED

You can connect and stay updated through Bart's website and social media:

Website: www.bartchristian.com.
Facebook fan page: facebook.com/wowbartchristian
Instagram: instagram.com/bartchristian1
LinkedIn: https://www.linkedin.com/in/bartchristian

ENDNOTES

1. Merriam-Webster's Dictionary *(online version)*, s.v. "delight (n.)," accessed at https://www.merriam-webster.com/dictionary/delight.
2. Dallan Forgaill, "Be Thou My Vision," accessed June 22, https://discoverpoetry.com/poems/dallan-forgaill/be-thou-my-vision/
3. Oxford English Dictionary Online, s.v. "blessing," accessed June 14, 2022, via Google search.
4. Merriam-Webster's Dictionary (online version), s.v. "delight (n)," accessed June 16, 2022, https://www.merriam-webster.com/dictionary/delight.
5. Merriam-Webster's Dictionary (online version), s.v. "fear (n.)," accessed June 16, 2022, https://www.merriam-webster.com/dictionary/fear.

6. Merriam-Webster's Dictionary (online version), s.v. "discernment (n.)," accessed June 16, 2022, https://www.merriam-webster.com/dictionary/discernment.

7. Merriam-Webster's Dictionary (online version), s.v. "trust (n.)," accessed June 16, 2022, https://www.merriam-webster.com/dictionary/trust.

8. U.S. Bureau of Labor Statistics, "American Time Use Survey, 2019 & 2020," https://www.bls.gov/tus/.

9. Helen Lemmel, "Turn Your Eyes Upon Jesus," 1922.

10. Dictionary.com, s.v. "always (adv.)," accessed June 16, 2022, https://www.dictionary.com/browse/always.

11. Dictionary.com, s.v. "advocate (n.)," accessed June 16, 2022, https://www.dictionary.com/browse/advocate.

12. Merriam-Webster's Dictionary (online version), s.v., "abundance (n.)," accessed June 16, 2022, https://www.merriam-webster.com/dictionary/abundance.

13. Merriam-Webster Online Dictionary (online version), s.v. "dull (adj.)," accessed June 16, 2022, https://www.merriam-webster.com/dictionary/dull

14. Helen Lemmel, "Turn Your Eyes Upon Jesus," 1922.

15. Robert Frost, "The Road Not Taken," 1915, accessed June 16, 2022, https://www.poetryfoundation.org/poems/44272/the-road-not-taken

Made in the USA
Middletown, DE
03 November 2022

13980135R00104